TRANSFORMATION

TRANSFORMATION

Autobiography of Beverly J. Vollmer (1937-2022)

Donna Costa, Editor

MITUAIGO BOOKS

Transformation: Autobiography of Beverly J. Vollmer (1937-2022)
Edited by Donna Costa
Published by MITUAIGO BOOKS
43 Shepherd Avenue
London, ON Canada N5V 4S3

PAPERBACK ISBN: 978-1-7774488-3-7

Front cover background photo by brett gaiser, Unsplash.

Connect with the Editor:
http://www.donnacosta.ca
https://www.facebook.com/AuthorDonnaCosta

First Edition, 2023

*To my children
and generations of the future.*

Contents

Foreword

When my mother (Beverly Vollmer) passed away in 2022, I placed a copy of her autobiography in the visitation room at the funeral home. The simple green binder from the dollar store was filled with Mom's stories – pages printed from her home computer, each painstakingly protected with a plastic sheath – and a scattering of timeless black and white photographs transporting us to another world, hinting at emotions of the past.

That green binder became a gathering point for friends and relatives as they scanned Mom's words. It helped release emotions and visitors' reminiscences about Mom, allowing the room to be filled with memories, laughter and, yes, tears.

Many asked where they could get a copy of Mom's autobiography to read. My siblings and I each had a typed binder copy (which we were hesitant to lend), but there was no master document. So I transferred the autobiography to a format we could then go ahead and self-publish. Thinking this would be a straight forward exercise – simply enter the existing data – I began the task. It didn't take long, however, for questions to arise. Do I correct spelling and grammatical errors? What about run-on sentences, conjunctions at the beginning of a sentence, repetitive use of words? Where full names were used, should I change them, abbreviate them, or leave as is? What about the use of words no longer politically correct?

So I consulted Susan L. Scott – the "L," I am convinced, must surely stand for *Lovely* – the editor of my short stories and novels. Susan, of course, as all lovely editors do, got precisely to the heart of the matter with her question, "If your mother were here and could OK the project, how would she want her work to be presented?"

Mom was once a typesetter at the local newspaper office. Her job included typing reports from local clubs about their activities, and she often commented how the spelling and grammar "needed fixing." Even though it wasn't her responsibility, Mom would make changes to the reports, as she couldn't stand to see the stories printed with errors.

Knowing Mom wouldn't want her work presented as anything less than her best, and knowing that none of us, including Mom, is perfect at grammar, I have made corrections only where necessary. In short, I have chosen to lightly edit her work for clarity, and to keep in mind that language and rules of grammar are evolving. For instance, one may now begin a sentence with a conjunction, drop commas, even – gasp – split an infinitive. After consideration, I have chosen to (mostly) leave Mom's words intact, even if they sometimes seem repetitive or not politically correct by today's standards. My choice has been to capture her personality, while reflecting her thinking and the language in use at that time. Although Mom was "a fuss-pot" about grammar, she was also without airs, admiring the relatable humour of Erma Bombeck and the ordinary women of Carol Shields' novels. My primary editing goal, then, has been to maintain Mom's own down-to-earth style.

Not wanting to surprise anyone who happens to appear in these pages, I have abbreviated, and sometimes changed, most names. All in all, I've tried to honour Mom's memory by keeping changes to a minimum. I hope Mom would be satisfied with the result.

Donna M. Costa *(nee Vollmer)*
March, 2023

Introduction

Just before Christmas, 1996, my daughter, Donna, came for a visit and brought along a tape recorder with a list of questions for me and my husband, Lorne, to answer, such as: When were you born? What was your childhood like? Tell us about your early years, etc.; her idea was for us to put our autobiographies on tape and to give one to each of the children for Christmas.

Although I thought it was a good idea at the time, I was too busy with the preparation and festivities of the Christmas season to carry out the project. But as of this year, March, 1988 (at age 61), I have retired from my position as a typesetter at *The Listowel Banner* and, after much contemplating, have decided to try my hand at writing a book.

This book, though, is not written with the intention of selling, but only to give my children and generations of the future, some insight into what the world was like during my life span and a bit of information about myself.

I never knew my maternal grandmother. She died when my mother was only 13. Nothing would be more gratifying to me now than to read a few words she had written when she was alive – a letter, or perhaps a few words written on a Christmas card, or maybe even a short note she may have hastily scribbled to a neighbour – so that I could know a little about her. But...I have nothing.

I want to leave a legacy when I exit this world; I want a part of me to remain long after I'm gone. Perhaps someday one of my great-great-great-grandkids should pick up this book and exclaim, "Hey, look at this! Did you know that great-great-great Grandma Vollmer lived in southern Ontario in the town of Listowel? And did you know she worked for many years for the local newspaper there? And it says here that she loved gardening, bowling and making teddy bears. She also had five children and they..." Then I will have accomplished what I set out to do in writing this book – to leave a part of myself and my family behind for my descendants. Although we'll never meet, my ancestors will have learned a bit about the era in which I lived.

I thank Donna for giving me the inspiration to write this book. I thank also my daughter, Charin, for giving me *Your Memoirs, History of Our Family,* and *Self Preservation,* three books which have helped me immensely in writing this autobiography. I thank her too, for urging me to the finish line.

Bev Vollmer

I

My Birth

I was born in Kitchener, Ontario, to Josephine and Norman Beilstein on October 28, 1937. I was the second of two children, my brother being three years older than me.

When my mother was pregnant with me, she and Dad lived in an apartment in Kitchener. Another woman in the apartment building was also pregnant and due around the same time as Mom. Each wondered who would have their baby first. It turned out that Mom and the other woman each delivered their babies the same day. Mom and Dad moved from that apartment shortly after my birth and lost touch with the other woman.

Then, years later when I was in Grade 6 and had just started at Sheppard School in Kitchener, the teacher checked for attendance and also asked the children for their birth date. One of the girls, Barbara Shoemaker, told the teacher her birthday was October 28, 1937 – same as mine. I also noticed she was left-handed – just like me. I thought this was quite a coincidence at the time, so of course when I got home from school, I immediately told Mom about her. Much to Mom's surprise – and mine – she said that Barbara was the daughter of the woman in her apartment who was expecting at the same time as her.

2

The Earliest Years

It has always intrigued me and aroused my curiosity of how far back in time one can remember. It seems strange too, that one can remember some things that happened 50 years ago, but can't remember what they did the week before (or in my case now, the day before!).

My earliest recollection of time was during World War II when my dad, who was a private and a cook in the army, was stationed at Camp Borden, Ontario. The year was 1942; I was five years old. Dad had a weekend leave and was coming home. I remember being on my tricycle in the middle of Shantz Lane, a long, gravel road on which we lived, and lined on both sides by trees, when I looked up and could see a man in uniform in the distance walking in my direction. I instinctively knew, as young as I was, that it was "my daddy" coming home. I jumped excitedly off my tricycle and raced as fast as I could into the house to tell Mother. I don't remember much more about that incident, except that my father brought home a rag doll for me to play with and a little cardboard table and chairs. It wasn't very expensive, I'm sure, but at the time I was as happy as someone who had just won the lottery.

I can still remember that doll. She had a stuffed, purple, polka-dot cloth body and head, but a papier-mâché face with big, bright, loveable brown eyes. I called her Sunbonnet Sue. I dragged that doll wherever I went; she became my constant travelling companion. When the fabric on the head started to wear thin, I asked my mother for an old pair of my long beige stockings, which were made of heavy cotton fabric. I remember cutting the stockings into small strips and attaching them to the fabric head with a needle and thread. I'm sure my sewing project was quite crude, but I admired my sewing skills at the time with much pride. Maybe that's where my love of sewing originated.

Eventually Sunbonnet Sue disappeared (probably to the scrap heap). I guess it was a time I was making a transition into another period of my life because I don't remember missing her or even asking about her. It was only after I had my own children that my memories of her came flooding back. Oh, how I wish I could say that my mother tucked her away in a trunk somewhere and I discovered her years later. But that wasn't meant to be.

3

My First Playmates

My first playmate that I can recall was Joan O. She had a hump back and was crippled and walked with braces, a result of contacting polio as a baby. As young as she was though, she was very aware of her deformities. I can remember her one day when her mother, Anne, was dressing her and Joan told me to look the other way because she didn't want me seeing her back without her blouse on.

One year when I was about five or six, Joan's father, John, bought a Model A Ford with a rumble seat, an outside seat that opened at the rear of the automobile. That fascinated me so much, as I had never seen a car before with a rumble seat. So you can imagine the thrill it was when John let Joan and me sit in the rumble seat while he took us on a tour around town. A rumble seat would be out of the question in cars today because of the high speeds on the highway, but back then cars never travelled too fast.

Joan had one brother, Kenneth, who was killed by a car when his mother sent him to the store on his bicycle to buy a loaf of bread. He was about eight years old. Sunnyside, where we lived, was a small community back then, and everyone felt a deep sense of loss and shock over the tragic event.

Another playmate back then whom I played with a lot was BarbaraL.

Her mother, I remember, gave us a snack each afternoon – a marmalade sandwich – which I hated, but ate anyway rather than offend her. To this day, I still dislike the taste of marmalade.

4

Christmas Time

One year when I was around six or seven years old, I got some sewing cards for Christmas. These were pictures on cardboard, with holes punched around the design and came with a needle and yarn. I thought that was the neatest present ever that year! My parents weren't fixed for money back then and couldn't afford much, but never once was I ever disappointed with what I received. Instead of buying one big expensive gift, my parents bought me a number of small inexpensive gifts, with my mother wrapping each one separately in colourful wrapping paper. As a kid, I never knew the value of a dollar and was always happy with what I received.

Christmas was a very happy time for me. I think I had just as much fun with those inexpensive gifts as today's kids have with their computer games, video sets, etc. Only once I remember being mildly disappointed when I asked for a china tea set and received a plastic one. My disappointment didn't last too long though, what with all the other gifts I got to open.

One thing I never tried to do though was to peek into my presents the way my own children now tell me they did when they were kids. I guess I enjoyed surprises much more than they did.

5

Going to School

The first school I attended was Sunnyside Public School on Weber Street in Kitchener. I went there for Grades 1 to 5. It was named Sunnyside after the area in which we lived, but later this area became known as the Kingsdale area. The year was 1943; I was almost six. It was a four-room school, with two grades in each class. When the bell rang each morning, we had to line up on each side of the school yard – boys on one side, girls on the other. We then sang "God Save the King" while the Union Jack was being raised up the flag pole, which sat in the centre of the front lawn. After that we lined up in pairs and marched into our rooms to the beat of the marching music being played on a gramophone inside the school.

I did fairly well at school in those early grades, getting good marks in all my subjects except geography and history. Oh, how I hated those two subjects. I usually did well in the written part of the exam, but when it came to putting places on a map, I always "blew" it. To this day, I have no sense of direction and am forever worrying about getting lost, which is one reason I never like to shop in a strange mall.

I enjoyed going to school in those early years, but occasionally it occurred to me now and then that I needed a holiday. That thought usually occurred on a Monday morning, which was one of Mom's washdays.

I don't know why, but there was something about the constant hum of the old washing machine in the kitchen, the rhythm of the music on the radio or listening to *Helen Trent* (Mom's favourite radio soap opera) and the peacefulness of the house that did something to me. Mondays were special days. Or maybe it was just being home alone with Mom that I enjoyed.

Anyway, there were more than a few times that I faked a stomach ache on a Monday morning so I could stay home. Mom would say, "Well, you go to school, Beverly, and if you get any worse, tell your teacher you're sick and come home." She was wise to me though and knew that once I got to school, I would be alright. Sometimes though I would cry, double over in pain and tell her "my stomach ache is so bad I can hardly walk." So then she'd send me to the couch to lie down until I felt better. Of course, I would go lie down until I thought school had started, then I'd suddenly announce I was feeling so much better and I'd start to play.

Boy, I sure enjoyed those Mondays at home with Mom!

6

School Concerts

One thing that especially stands out in my mind is the Christmas concerts that were held at Sunnyside School each Christmas. Unlike in the schools today where only some children get to play a part, each child back then had a part to play in the concert (sometimes two or three). The two parts I remember being in were (a) when I was in Grade 1 and my classmates and I put on a skit of the nursery rhyme "Hey Diddle Diddle." I was to be the dog in the skit. While the teacher read the part "And the little dog laughed," I was supposed to come out on the stage from behind the curtain wearing a dog face that I had made out of a paper bag. But just before I was to make my debut, I peeked between the stage curtains and saw all the people in the audience. I was so petrified that I ran out on the stage holding my dog face in my hand and then just as quickly ran back again behind the curtain.

And (b) another time when I was in Grade 2, some of the children in my class had to perform a Dutch dance. The teacher paired me off with David W., a cute little boy in my class that I had a real crush on. We had many practices before the final concert and, needless to say, I enjoyed every one of them. (Whether David shared the same enthusiasm though was never established.)

And, of course, the most exciting part of the concerts (at least when

I was in the early grades) was when Santa made his appearance. I remember how he always came through a window at the back of the stage. Feelings of tension, anxiety and happiness were all rolled together as I waited for that magic moment to arrive. (Ah, to be a child again!)

7

Miss King

Miss King was my Grade 5 teacher. For some reason (unknown to me now), I disliked her intensely from the beginning. But because of an incident that happened while I was in her class, my dislike of her eventually turned to "despised."

One day in class, I printed on a piece of paper "Miss King is a dirty nut" and passed it around the room. When one of my classmates – Mark P. – read it, he took it upon himself to present it to the teacher. Miss King read the note and then asked the class who wrote it. Of course, I sat innocently at my desk, staring into space, letting on I didn't know what she was talking about, until she said, "Beverly, did you write this note?" I stammered, "Yes" to her and was told to come to the front of the class. She then pulled up a chair and placed it in the centre of the room and sat down. Then she took me over her knee, pulled up my dress in front of the class, revealing my underwear, and spanked me. I was humiliated beyond belief.

My cousin, Phyllis, was in the same grade as I was, so it didn't take long for her to relate the story to the rest of my family. She had promptly gone home after school and told her mom, and then Aunt Effie phoned my mom. I had to relive the humiliation all over again when Mom asked me for details.

The irony of it all though was that when I married Lorne and we settled into our first home, Miss King lived two doors down. Even after all those years, I still found her repulsive, and could barely manage a decent "hello" in passing her on the street.

8

The House on Shantz Lane

Over the eight years I went to public school, my family moved around a lot, but stayed in the Kingsdale area, just a different house. The first home I remember was the one on Shantz Lane. This was a three-room house with no indoor plumbing. The bathroom (referred to as the outhouse) was outside, but a pot under the bed substituted for the "real thing" many a time. A pump in the kitchen was used for pumping water.

On wash days, Mom had to pump water into pails, heat the water on the stove and then fill up the washing machine before starting the wash. After the clothes were washed, they had to be put through the wringer into another tub of warm water, swished around a bit, and then put through the wringer again and into the clothes basket. No easy task, I must say. I did the wash the same way myself for about the first seventeen or eighteen years of my marriage (except I didn't have to heat the water). After the clothes were washed, they had to be hung outside. (No such thing as a dryer in those days either!) In winter, the clothes were left in the basket to thaw out for a while to make them more pliable for a second hanging indoors.

Bath time was only once a week – Saturday night. In between, we had sponge baths in a basin. When Saturday night came, Mom pulled out the galvanized steel tub and set it in the kitchen. Again, she had to heat the water for the bath. Then my brother got the first bath; when he was done, I was next to go in, in the same water. I enjoyed the bath time though, because Mom always washed the bedding on Saturday mornings and then put the freshly washed sheets back on the bed before bedtime, making sure to fold the top sheet back over the blankets, which made the bed look very appealing. It was so nice after having a warm bath to crawl under those clean, fragrantly sweet-smelling bed sheets.

Another thing I remember about the house on Shantz lane was a trap door in the middle of the kitchen floor. I can't remember ever going to the basement, which makes me believe that there was no basement under the house, only a dugout for storing things. Behind the house was our outhouse and also a shed where Dad kept his hounds. We had a cat back then, too, and one year she had kittens in another part of the shed, away from the dogs, but the day after they were born, they magically disappeared. Dad thought maybe the old Tom cat killed them or maybe the mother carried them off to another place.

9

The House on Weber Street

By the time I started school, my parents decided to sell and build a new house. They bought a lot on Weber Street, almost directly across from Sunnyside School in the Kingsdale area. Dad made the decision then to build the house himself. He worked almost every night and weekends to have the house ready by the time we had to leave the old house on Shantz Lane. But I guess he knew the house wouldn't be finished on time, so we rented rooms in a house on Prospect Avenue, which was directly behind the school, until the house was finished. We lived there only for a few months.

Our backyard on Weber Street butted against the backyard of the Lutheran Church. Although we belonged to the church, we never went too often, so we never knew what was going on in the parish. One spring, Dad decided to order a load of manure for our garden, and it just happened that the very day the manure arrived was the same day that the church was having their strawberry social (in the backyard of the church, of course). I don't think the congregation thought too much of Dad that day, but we had a lot of laughs over it.

Another thing I remember about that house was roller skating in the basement. I used to zip around from room to room, pretending I was a famous skater. I spent hours roller skating around that basement, as there were no sidewalks in Kingsdale at that time. On a few occasions when we went to Grampa Zmija's house on Pinke Street in Kitchener (now Weber Street), I would take my roller skates and skate around the block while I was there.

We lived in that house for about five years before leaving the Kingsdale area and moving to Sydney Street in Kitchener. That meant starting a new school and leaving my old friends behind, which didn't appeal to me at all.

10

The House on Sydney Street

We lived on Sydney Street for the next two years, and I can honestly say that I haven't many happy memories of that place. For one thing, I hated the new school (Sheppard School) that I had to attend. I never did seem to fit in with the other kids there. To begin with, I was painfully shy around these new kids and I missed all my old friends from the Kingsdale area. Most of the kids at Sheppard School came from rich Jewish families (or so I thought at the time), and I didn't seem to fit in with them. I attended Grade 6 and 7 there.

I did become friends with one new girl, Marian W., who went to the same church as me, and we had many happy times together, especially the couple of summers we attended church camp for a week up at Goderich. Marian and I remained friends through our school years, even after my family moved from that area.

After we each married and had families, we visited back and forth for quite a while, but then eventually lost touch with each other. Marian had married a guy that stuttered very bad. It was embarrassing whenever they came for a visit because neither Lorne nor I could understand him. Later, after they had children, one of the children picked up his speech impediment and stuttered as bad as he did.

It was while living on Sydney Street that I first learned to ride a

19

two-wheeler. Dad said he'd show me how and proceeded to teach me on my brother's bicycle. Up the road a ways was a very bumpy, gravel-lined hill which led into a farmer's field. Dad took to the top of the hill, set me on the bicycle seat, then informed me to steer after he gave me a push. Well, I hardly got started down the hill when I slid off the seat onto the cross bar. I rode that bar all the way to the bottom of the hill, hitting every bump along the way, until the bike flipped over at the bottom and I crash-landed onto the gravel. Needless to say, I wasn't too keen on ever getting on a bicycle for a long time after that. (It surprises me yet that I was able to have children after that!)

It was while living on Sydney Street that my brother died from bone cancer at the age of 15. I was 12 years old and in Grade 7 at the time. I remember that day vividly. I was playing with Karen S., a girl with whom I went to school. She lived on Sheldon Avenue in a house that was directly behind ours.

Dad came over and said he wanted me home right away. As I walked back to our house along with Dad, one of the neighbours hollered over. "Oh, Mr. Beilstein," she said, "How is your son doing?" Dad didn't answer, just kept on going. I remember looking up at him and saying, "Hey, Dad, Mrs. (so and so) asked you how Donnie was." He didn't answer me, just kept on walking toward our house. I couldn't figure out why he wasn't talking.

It was only after we returned home I found out why. Donnie had died. After his death, Mom and Dad couldn't bear to live in the same house anymore and quickly sold it and moved back to the Kingsdale area, this time to a house on Second Avenue.

II

Dolly

I started Grade 8 while living on Second Avenue, but not at Sunnyside School. Since more people were living in that area now, Sunnyside School was filled to capacity, so the Grade 8s had to go by bus to Victoria School in Kitchener.

During my year in Grade 8, I met a girl named Dolly S. I only knew her for one year, but she left a lasting impression on me. Her real name was Dolores, but everyone called her "Dolly" which was nothing like what her name implied.

In 1988, while taking a correspondence English course, I wrote a short story about her. Here is that story:

> I remember Dolly as though it were yesterday. She was my friend back in the eighth grade. She was everybody's friend, never having an enemy in the world.
>
> Outwardly, Dolly was not pretty as her name might imply. She was a skinny, freckled-face kid with overly fuzzy, short blond hair, the result of too many home perms, and she was very round-shouldered. Her knee socks, which were popular wearing apparel back then, were always twisted down around her ankles and her

tunics were always too long or too short, whatever was not in fashion at the time. And she had a tomboyish mannerism about her, a trait not really suitable for a girl entering puberty.

But Dolly possessed something that most people take a lifetime to acquire. She possessed an inner beauty that could equal the best of Rembrandt's paintings. When Dolly walked into a room, the room instantly brightened. It came to life, her warm personality enveloping the entire class. The "Sunshine Girl" I secretly called her.

Dolly's zest for living was contagious. Even though I haven't seen her since graduating from the eighth grade thirty-six years ago, at times I can still feel her presence. When I'm feeling down, I think of Dolly and my spirits rise, which tells me that Dolly is out there somewhere, still spreading her sunshine.

12

First Date

Back in Grade 8, my two closest friends were Joyce W. and Janet H. Having gone all through public school together, we had had many fun times over the years. At 13, we were at that age when girls notice boys, and vice versa. It was this attraction to the opposite sex that led us on our first real date – together! Of course, we had had boyfriends before this, but never had a date with a guy who actually owned a car.

It was Good Friday, 1951, and we were out of school for Easter break. With spring in the air and boredom setting in, we decided to take a stroll to the Rockway, which was about a mile's walk from home.

It wasn't long before a car pulled up with three good-looking guys in it and started to talk to us. Well, at first, we ignored them, but soon a conversation evolved. Before long, they asked us to go for a ride, and after much whispering amongst us girls while the car drove along beside us, we decided to accept. I jumped in beside the driver, Rusty E. (I thought he was the best looking), while Joyce jumped in beside me. Janet was left to sit in the back with Ronnie W. and Melvin E., Rusty's brother. Somehow or other, I can't remember how, before the night ended, we paired off – me with Rusty, Joyce with Ronny, and Janet with Melvin.

It was on this date that I had my first taste of liquor. While the six of us were all piled in the car together (no seatbelt laws back then), one of the guys passed a mickey of whiskey around. Not wanting to feel like a nerd, I took a good swig from the bottle and almost gagged when the whiskey hit my throat. Needless to say, it was a long time after that before I touched whiskey again.

For the next year or so, Rusty and I dated quite frequently, usually taking in many drive-in movies, which were very popular at the time, and also because Rusty never liked dancing. Joyce and Ronnie dated a lot, too, but Janet and Melvin never dated again after that first night.

Joyce has remained one of my best friends through the years. She married Lavern H. and they have travelled extensively over the years, living for a few years in England and then moving back to Toronto where Lavern set up a publishing business.

After selling the business many years later, they moved to Peterborough into a beautiful lake-front home. They have since moved into a beautiful home in New Hamburg in a seniors' subdivision. My husband and I still keep in touch with them and have had many good times together over the years.

EDITOR'S NOTE: Bev and Joyce remained in touch through emails, cards at Christmas and birthdays, and regular phone calls right up until Joyce's passing five months before Bev.

13

Other Memories

Money was tight when I was a child, but we never went hungry. I remember Mom telling me that one Christmas when we kids were small, there wasn't enough money to buy a turkey for Christmas, so she went out and bought a head of cabbage and a few pounds of hamburger and made cabbage rolls, along with the usual mashed potatoes, vegetables and gravy. As kids, we didn't know any different and enjoyed the cabbage rolls just as well as turkey.

Apple crisp and raisin squares were another specialty of Mom's. She made them a lot and I sure did love them! Calories didn't concern me much back then – and it showed. I was quite chubby until I reached Grade 6 when a Mennonite girl, Miriam G., told me I was the fattest kid in our class.

I had asked her if I was as fat as Karen, a girlfriend of mine, and Miriam laughed and said, "You're fatter than her. You're the fattest kid in the class!" Well, those words really stung, especially when you're just a kid in Grade 6. After that, I became more aware of food and watched what I was eating.

I remember when I was in Grade 1 or 2, Mom occasionally would give me a nickel to go to the store after school to buy a couple of two-cent grab bags (a mixture of different candies), and then she'd remind me to bring home the change.

I remember when every home had an ice box to keep food cold. The iceman came once or twice a week and would bring in a huge block of ice and put it in the top of the ice box. While the iceman was delivering the ice to the household, we kids in the neighbourhood would jump on the back of the truck and gather up the tiny bits of ice that had broken off. We thought sucking on that was a great treat! When the iceman came back out of the house, we kids would run like heck, thinking that if he caught us, we would surely catch hell.

We also had a baker who came once or twice a week. He came with a horse and cart, filled with different breads and pastries. Mom would purchase what she needed for a couple days until he came again. I remember Mom often buying the maple tarts – a tart with a jam base and covered with a cake-like batter, followed by a topping of maple icing. Boy, I sure did love them!

And every so often the ragman, as we kids called him, would go around to the houses with his horse and cart looking for just about anything that you had to give him. As a kid, I was always terrified when I saw him coming and would hide somewhere until he left.

Then there was the milkman. Every house had a milk box attached to it, near the back door, much like homes today have a mailbox, only the milk box was bigger. Mom would make out a list of how many quarts of milk or cream or butter that she wanted and then leave a note in the milk box for the milkman.

Joyce F. was a girl with whom I attended grade school. Occasionally, Mom would let her sleep over at our house, although Mom never liked Joyce – Mom thought Joyce was too giddy. As Mom said to me once after one of these sleepovers, "You two giggled all night."

As a kid, we never got to go too many places, other than visit relatives. And in those days, you never visited them without an invitation. And when you did, you behaved – or else you heard about it later! I did go to the circus every year though, which I thoroughly enjoyed.

Maybe it was because my grandfather had been a circus performer in his younger years that I received that privilege.

14

❦

My Mother

To describe a family member is very hard indeed, as I found out trying to describe my mother.

Mom was born Josephine Helen Zmija, in Kitchener, Ontario, on June 16, 1913. She died on January 17, 1995, at 82, during a church service in Caressant Care Nursing Home, Listowel, Ontario. This always seemed a bit ironic to me since Mom never attended church too often, believing that a Christian is determined not by how often one attends church, but how one lives day-to-day. (And I have to admit that I agree somewhat with that philosophy myself.) She was one of two children, her brother, Joe, being three years younger than she was.

The day before Mom died, we had had a terrible ice storm. The streets and sidewalks in Listowel were treacherous – complete sheets of ice. At that time, I was working at *The Listowel Banner* (the town's newspaper), and could barely make my way after work to the parking lot to get into my car without crawling on my hands and knees. As I sat in the car, I debated about going over to Caressant Care to feed Mom her supper as I usually did every day after work. Just getting home, I knew, would be a chore.

But the thought occurred to me that the only thing Mom had to look forward to was my coming to visit. If I didn't come, I knew they

29

(the nurses) would probably feed her a few mouthfuls and then whisk her off to her room to bed. So I went over and fed her supper. Mom generally took at least an hour to eat, as did many of the other residents there, but the nurses, I was told, were to have all the residents in and out of the dining area in one hour. I honestly believe that if one doesn't have a family member to look out for them, they'll never survive very long in a nursing home (or a hospital either, for that matter). But that's another story.

Anyway, around noon the next day, I received a call from the doctor telling me in a very nonchalant way (or so I thought at the time) that Mom had passed away earlier in the morning during the church service. I was devastated. I wondered why the doctor or one of the nursing home staff hadn't phoned earlier to tell me she had had a heart attack. Why did they wait for two hours before phoning me? I am thankful though that I did go over the night before and had one last visit with her, or I never would have been able to live with myself.

Mom was a shy, quiet person who loved the simple things in life, such as gardening, sewing on her old treadle machine or cleaning around the house (something she did with real vigour – her house was always spotless). Rather than spend an afternoon drinking tea with the neighbours, as many of the housewives did in those days, she spent it working at something around the house. But this wasn't to say that she was snooty, as she did have many chats over the backyard fence with her neighbours; Mom just never did much socializing with anyone.

Mom and Dad were friends with one couple, Isabelle and Harold. They had one daughter, Darlene, and visited with us many times over the years. Isabelle and Harold are both gone now, too, but Darlene and I (even though we haven't seen each other for forty or so years), still keep in touch with each other via a Christmas card every year.

Mom was a person very dedicated to her family. When my brother and I left for school in the morning and when we came home after school, she was always there for us. She always had good nutritious meals on the table, nursed us through our childhood illnesses, patched and washed our clothes, cleaned up after us many times, and also packed my clothes when I went off to summer camp in Goderich for a week. She wrote me a letter every day while I was there. I was the only kid at camp who received mail every day. I think she must have written and mailed the letters before I even left for camp because I received one every day while I was there, right up until the last day.

As a kid, I can remember lying on the floor while Mom sewed on her old Singer, and I'd complain of having nothing to do. She'd say, "Why don't you write all the words you can think of starting with 'b' or 'c'" or whatever. So I'd get out the paper and pencil and sit there for hours trying to think of all the words starting with that letter.

When I finished, Mom would look at my list and praise me for having such a long list. Of course, I loved the praise and felt so proud, not realizing that she only told me to write the list so as to keep me from getting bored. This happened many times during summer vacation, but I never tired of the game.

Mom never had much of an education; she only went as far as Grade 8 in school. I really don't think this bothered her though, as she seemed very content with her lot in life. She could read and write very well, just skipped the big words she didn't know. She never read novels, but did read lots of magazines and always took time to read *The Kitchener Record*.

And she loved watching old movies. You could ask her anything about old-movie stars, such as Betty Grable, Lana Turner, Jane Powell, Humphrey Bogart or Clark Gable, or any of the old vaudeville stars, and she always managed to tell you a tidbit or two about them. In fact, I think she relished all the questions asked, as being able to relay a few facts of their lives gave her a sense of importance.

Something Mom had was heaps of patience. If she started something, she always finished it, no matter how long it took to complete. If she had to do something over or rip something out while she was sewing, she would do it. Quitting was unheard of to her. And no matter how mad or irritated she was, Mom never swore.

When Dad died in1973, Mom was determined she was going to learn to drive. Three years later, at the age of 63, she went out and bought a fire red 1976 Chevette and signed up for driving lessons. After about six or seven driving tests, she finally got her license. I think she deserved a lot of credit for learning to drive at 63. I know if I had to learn to drive now, I couldn't do it. Her persistence was incredible!

Mom though, like all of us, wasn't perfect; she did have some weird quirks at times, like when she bought her Chevette. For some reason, she had the notion that the gas tank should always be full. She would drive to the HiWay Market which was only a five-minute drive from her home, get her groceries, and then stop at the service station on the way back and tell the attendant to "fill 'her up.'" The first time this happened, the attendant told her that there must be something wrong with her gas gauge as the tank was already full. But Mom would insist he add some more anyway to make it completely full. I'm sure the attendant must have rolled his eyes around at that request.

When Mom started having problems with her walking, I would drive down from Listowel to Kitchener and take her shopping once a week. But Mom always wanted me to drive her car to the HiWay Market, then insisted that I fill up with gas on the way home. When I refused, knowing the gas tank was already over three-quarters full, Mom got mad and we always wound up in an argument. Mom had a habit, too, of vacuuming and washing the car every week, even though it never was dirty.

Another time, my Uncle Walter, who had studied taxidermy, had given my dad some birds that he had mounted. They were in a glass showcase and were exquisitely beautiful. For reasons unknown to me, my mother gave them to the Salvation Army after my father died. When my uncle eventually asked for them after my father's death, my mother told him she no longer had them. He was absolutely furious when she told him she gave them away. If I had known she was going to give them away, I would have asked for them myself. When Mom got a notion to throw something out though, she did; she couldn't stand clutter.

Another time, she threw out a huge fish that Dad had mounted, which he had caught on one of his many fishing trips. I was very upset over this, as it would have been a wonderful memento of him now, and also something to show my children and grandchildren.

Yes, Mom had faults, but I loved her – faults and all – but never told her so in all my 58 years with her. This is one thing I deeply regret. Now it is too late. So, if you have a loved one – a parent, husband, wife, or children – tell them how much you love them before it is too late!

15

My Father

Dad was born Norman William Beilstein on April 27, 1910, in Hanover, Ontario. He was the youngest of ten children. Two of his sisters, Edith and Viola, died at exactly eight months, eight days of age and within nine years of each other.

After a stint in the army around 1942, Dad worked for a while as a cook at a restaurant – The Castle Inn – in Kitchener. But the hours were long and tedious, so eventually he quit. After that, he worked in a rubber factory for a while, but eventually quit there and landed a job at J.M. Schneiders in Kitchener where he worked until his death on February 21, 1973.

While he was still single, Dad worked with a guy named Harold. Each knew the other was getting married, but neither would reveal their wedding date to the other when asked. Harold and Dad made a bet with each other over who would get married first but, as it turned out, they both got married the same day, December 2, 1933. Harold married a woman named Isabelle and, of course, Dad married my mother, Josephine Zmija. Mom was 20 and Dad, 23. They were married by Rev. C.F. Barthel in Kitchener, Ontario. Isabelle and Harold remained life-long friends with Mom and Dad, and all spent their entire lives in Kitchener. Harold also worked at J.M. Schneiders until his death.

Dad was an avid sportsman who enjoyed hunting and fishing. I remember, as a kid, there was always a hound or two in a pen out the back. Dad's favourite hound, though, was a dog named Goldie. I think I got my love and compassion for animals from Dad, as he was always caring and protective toward animals and he could never stand anyone being cruel to them.

Dad went on many fishing trips over the years, but there's one I can remember quite well, as I went along on that trip. Dad was going ice fishing with a guy named Lloyd R. and some other guy and decided to take me along with them. I remember we had to travel a long distance to our destination, but finally we got there and were ready to fish. But just moments onto the ice, I somehow fell through and got soaked to the skin, so everyone had to pack up his gear again and head for home. I'm sure the guys with Dad were furious with me that day! I don't really know Lloyd very well, but twice now I have met him at funerals in Hesson, Ontario, where he came over and recounted that story to me. Lloyd passed away this year, 1999.

Dad spent many hours playing with me as a child. It was Dad who taught me how to ride a two-wheeler and to play checkers, darts and ping pong. (I could play ping pong for hours – I loved it!) It was Dad who taught me how to put a worm on a hook, how to fish, how to cast my rod.

It was Dad who taught me how to tell time when the teacher sent a note home with me in Grade 1 asking my parents to help me because I couldn't seem to grasp the reasoning of it all. I remember Dad making a clock out of a paper plate and explaining over and over again that when the hand was on the right side, it was "after" the hour, and when it was the left side, it was "to" the hour. At six years of age, the complexity of the lesson seemed so overwhelming, until finally, like a burst bubble, it instantly became clear and I wondered why I was so stupid and hadn't gotten it sooner. It was Dad, too, who helped me with my homework and shared his love of country music with me.

In his younger days, Dad taught guitar lessons. When I was about eight, he decided to teach me. I got pretty proficient at playing "Nearer

My God To Thee" when something broke on the guitar and that was the end of my lessons. I can't remember if Dad ever got that guitar fixed or not, but at that point in time, I wasn't too keen on learning to play it anyway, although I wish now that I could.

I don't want it to sound here as though my mother never played games with me or took time to do things with me, because she did, many times. But as a mother, she was busy a lot – preparing meals, cleaning the house, sewing, mending our clothes, etc. – doing all the chores that comes with being a mom.

When Dad died from a heart attack at age 63 on February 21, 1973, I felt like a part of me had died too. I had been working that day at Spinrite Yarns in Listowel. I was on the 3 to 11 pm shift and had had a great day at work. I was in an extremely happy mood as I walked in the back door after work and heard the phone ring. When I answered it, Mom spoke and asked to speak to Lorne. I could tell by her trembling voice that something was wrong, but I didn't ask questions, just handed the phone over to Lorne. When Lorne got off the phone, he told me Dad had died from a massive heart attack.

Dad had had a heart attack weeks earlier and had been hospitalized and then sent home to rest. He was told not to exert himself in any way. But the day he died, he felt pretty good in the morning so, around supper time, he decided to blow out the snow from his drive. Mom was worried about him though, so she went outside with him. After he blew the snow from his own drive, he decided to blow out the neighbour's drive too, since the neighbour, Earl, had done Dad's drive while he was in the hospital. He had just started on Earl's drive when he took a massive heart attack and died instantly in front of Mom. An ambulance was called, but he was dead on arrival at the hospital.

My world crashed that night, and it has taken me a long time to get over Dad's death. I thought that, like God, Dad was invincible.

It still seems ironic to me that when Lorne and I went to Mom's the next morning after Dad had died, I found Dad's whiskey glass still on the cupboard. It read, "One for the road."

16

My Brother

When Donna first asked me to write my autobiography, one of her requests was that I tell something about my brother. What was he like? What were his hobbies? Who were his friends? I wish I could comply with that request, but I can't. The truth of the matter is that I remember very little about my brother. I really believe now that when he died at the age of 15, my body went into shock and I lost all memory of him. I was 12 when he died, old enough that I should be able to remember visiting relatives with him, going to the circus with him, family discussions, where he sat at the table, etc., and yet I can't remember anything. Until now, I have never told anyone this except my friends, Ivan and Dorothy, when Lorne and I were in Vegas with them and I had one too many whiskeys. Lorne wasn't in the room at the time and even he doesn't know what I am about to write here, as I have never been able to talk about my brother with anyone.

When I was about 10 or 11, my brother got bone cancer. My parents told me Donny was sick, but never told me what he had, probably thinking I was too young to understand. I never questioned my parents on the subject and they never volunteered any more information, maybe too because they didn't want me (or my brother) to know the seriousness of his illness. I do remember him often being in the Sick

Children's Hospital in Toronto, and I can remember waiting in the car many times while my parents took him to a "charm" doctor some place around Waterloo Park in Kitchener to try and cure him. My parents also had a tutor come to the house on a weekly visit so my brother could catch up with his studies.

The few things I do remember about my brother are these...

His favourite singer was Al Jolson, a blues singer.

Donny always wanted to take a Charles Atlas course, although I can't remember him ever doing so. In those days, Charles Atlas was a fictitious character that appeared in every comic book ad. He would be depicted in one picture as a scrawny, little guy at the beach that all the touch guys picked on; in the next picture, after he had taken a Charles Atlas course, he was shown at the beach with bulging muscles, looking like Arnold Schwarzenegger, and with a bevy of girls flocking around him.

I think my brother wanted to take the course because there were two bullies in his class that were forever picking on him in school – Bobby S. and Richard B. – and I think this really bothered him. Robby and Richard were unusually big for their age and liked to bully the other kids around. Donny was a Grade A student, always passing at the top of his class, and because of this, Bobby and Richard named him B-B Brain, which also bothered Donny. At summer camp one year in Goderich, Donny phoned home mid-week for Mom and Dad to come and get him because Bobby and Richard tormented him all the time he was there. It was ironic to me years later while going through the visitation book from Donny's funeral that Richard and Bobby both attended the funeral home visitation.

Donny's best friend was Ronald Fry, also an A student and at the top of the class. Although they were always competing for first place, I don't think they were ever jealous of each other.

When we lived on Weber Street, my brother raised homing pigeons. Dad built a shed out the back for them and used to buy straw from a farmer, Mr. Shue, for bedding the birds.

Donny was born September 27, 1934, and died June 11, 1949, at the age of 15. He was the only one to carry the Beilstein name into the next generation. One of Dad's four brothers, Nelson, was the only one who had children, both girls. Dad's sisters had boys but, of course, they took their husband's name after they married.

The night before Donny died, he had a terrible bloody nose. Mom was rushing around the bathroom looking after him. I remember at one point asking for something and Mom hollering at me, "Don't bother me now, I'm busy with Donny." I remember screaming, "Just because he's a little bit sick, he gets all the attention!"

Donny was rushed to the hospital later that night and died the next day. I have to live with those words now for the rest of my life, something I regret saying a million times over.

After he died, whenever Mom tried to talk to me about Donny, I would clam up and refuse to speak until she changed the subject. Even after I married, I could never bring myself to talk to my parents or husband, or anyone for that matter, about Donny. When Mom in her later years went into the nursing home, she took all the family pictures that she had on the wall except Donny's even though it was the only enlargement she had of him. And I know she did this for a reason – to make sure that I would always have a picture to remember him by.

17

Grandma and Grandpa Zmija

I don't have many memories of my grandparents except that of my maternal grandfather, Vincent Zmija, my mother's father. He was born in Poland in 1888 and died in Kitchener, Ontario, in 1966, at age 78. He was employed as a cabinet maker by Krug Furniture Co. Ltd. in Kitchener for 40 years.

As I said earlier at the beginning of this autobiography, my maternal grandmother died at a young age, when my mother was only 13. Her death is still a mystery to me, as I have heard so many rumours from different relatives. I don't know which to believe. My mother said she was told by her father that her mother died when she went up to the attic to get something and the trap door to the attic fell down on her head.

Another time, I asked my Aunt Paula if she knew. Paula was my mother's brother's wife. Paula had a different story to tell, saying that Joe, my mother's brother, told her that his mother died of an illness.

Another time, I asked Mom's cousin if he knew what my grandmother had died from and he said she had had an abortion and died from it. My mother was 13 at the time of her mother's death and Joe would have been 10. I guess I'll never know the truth because there's no one left to ask.

My grandmother was born Mary Mikolajczuk in 1891 and died in 1927. She is buried in Mount Hope Cemetery in Kitchener, Ontario.

My grandfather had come to Kitchener from Poland with my grandmother shortly after their marriage, leaving from the Port of Bremer Haven, and settling in the Kitchener-Waterloo area. They had two children, my mother, Josie, and Joe.

After my grandmother died, my grandfather eventually remarried Michalina Kubasiak who had three children, two from her first husband (a man by the last name Targosz) and one from my grandfather's brother.

Grandad and his second wife lived on Pinke Street (now Weber St.) in Kitchener for many years until poor health forced him to move to Freeport Hospital where he later died. I never did like my step-grandmother very much, as she always seemed to favour her real grandchildren over me. She was born in 1896 and died April 9, 1983, and is buried in Woodland Cemetery, Kitchener, Ontario, alongside my grandfather.

I can remember on some occasions, my grandfather would sneak me a quarter or 50 cents, and tell me in his broken English not to mention it to Grandma. A few times she caught him giving me money and then she would argue with him in Polish. As young as I was, I knew she was mad at him for giving me money. A few times at Christmas though, we went to their house and a lot of mom's relatives were there – all cousins – and I really had a great time.

My cousins – Joanne, Karen and Junior – and I would put on a Christmas concert and then pass the hat around for a collection. We would do silly things, like reading a poem or something stupid, or sometimes Joanne would sing a song. We would collect a few nickels and dimes and thought we were in seventh heaven. We had a great time doing that at Christmas. I'm sure the adults weren't too happy about watching our performance though, and probably wished we'd beat it so they could talk.

18

Grandma and Grandpa Beilstein

I only have a few memories of Grandma and Grandpa Beilstein, my paternal grandparents. Grandma Beilstein was born Adeline C. Eidt on March 28, 1870, and died August 12, 1948, at 78 years. She was a small woman who, as I remember, had white hair and always wore it pulled into a bun at the back. My memories of Grandpa Beilstein are vague, except for one recollection I have of visiting him when he was sick in bed. He died shortly after that visit.

Grandma and Grandpa lived in a rambling big house on Benton Street in Kitchener. There was a large kitchen at the back of the house and a dining room off the kitchen, towards the front of the house. Another doorway off the kitchen, towards the back of the house, led to a closed-in room of some sorts, which led to the attic. Upstairs was the bathroom, where a large stuffed owl sat on a dresser in one of the bedrooms. When I was a child, every time I had to pass that room to use the bathroom, I would see those large eyes of the owl looking at me and it frightened me very much.

Down the hall at the front of the house was a parlour, and the only time we kids were allowed in there was at Christmas. That room always held an aura of mystery to me for that reason, but I loved going there at Christmas. Grandma kept a small decorated tree on a table in there. It wasn't much, but to me it seemed special. The room looked so inviting with the shiny hardwood floors and everything so neat and immaculate.

I can't remember, though, ever getting a Christmas present from any of my grandparents. Grandma and Grandpa Beilstein had a large family of ten children and money wasn't very plentiful, even though only one daughter, my Aunt Mamie, still remained at home by the time I was three or four years old.

Grandpa Beilstein was a great circus performer before he met my grandmother. He did an aerial act where he built a pyramid with chairs forty-feet high and then would climb to the top and stand on his head. It was a magnificent act and, as I was told years ago by my brother-in-law, my grandfather's name is listed in the Circus Hall of Fame somewhere in the USA. My brother-in-law happened to be there and saw the same picture that we had in our possession which my husband and I had shown him at one time.

Being a circus performer in those days was not considered a stable occupation to be in. When Grandpa married Grandma and they had children, Grandma insisted that he never talk to the children about his life in the circus. But I think that when Grandma was out of ear shot, Grandpa let a few secrets out of the bag to his children, and they were mighty proud of him.

While he was in the circus, Grandpa went by the stage name of Mons-Natalie. I have a photocopy of a letter that he wrote to his sister from Chicago. It is dated June 8, 1890. It shows his aerial act to the left and above the letter it reads:

From the Hippodrome Paris, France. The Grecian champion equilibrist and marvel of all Europe in his inimitable and unapproachable acts of equilibrium on self-constructed pyramids forty feet high, the most startling and daring act ever introduced in this country. Permanent address, Care, New York Clipper

Below the illustration it reads:

No illustration can do this act justice, and the above sketches but faintly outline the dangerous and unusually thrilling character of the performance I give, but they are taken from instantaneous photographs and are, therefore, neither imaginary or exaggerated. In addition to the feats of balancing, I am an all around performer, and the only man that can do the wonderful Spanish ring act.

The letter itself reads:

Chicago, June 8th, 1890

Dear Sister,

With pleasure I write these few lines to you to let you know that I have come to Chicago again to my old homestead as I like it better here and better business. I am also in good state of health at present as I was sick of New York and could not do business there so I am going to try it again here. I have not a great deal to say for this time, excuse me. Hoping that youse are all well.

Your brother,
William

Grandpa Beilstein was born October 18, 1850, and died December 3, 1942. Grandpa and Grandma Beilstein are both buried in Woodland Cemetery, Kitchener, Ontario. They had ten children, but two daughters died in infancy and are buried in Hanover, Ontario.

Grandpa Beilstein's parents, my great grandparents, were Phillip and Johnetta Beilstein and are also buried in Hanover Cemetery.

19

High School

I started high school in September, 1951, at Kitchener-Waterloo Collegiate (KCI). Much of my high school days is a blur to me, as I only attended for Grade 9 and for two months of Grade 10. During that time, about my only goal in life was to quit school and get a job. Back then the schools didn't prepare girls for occupations as they did boys. Girls usually worked for a while after they finished high school, then eventually married and had children. Not many women worked outside the home then as women do today.

Two subjects I really liked in high school were English and Home Economics. One time in English class, we had a contest in which we had to write a five-minute essay on the subject of our choice. We had to read it in front of the class, and then the class had a vote to see whose essay was the best. The person whose essay was chosen then had to compete against the other Grade 9 classes.

Well, I remember writing about a dog and ending my story with something like "Even now, I don't know if it was Coke spilled on the rug or something else" or something to that effect, insinuating that maybe the dog had peed on the rug. The class laughed like heck at my ending and chose me to be the one to compete against the other Grade 9s. But not before the teacher took me aside and told me I had better change the ending. I guess he didn't think it was proper for me to insinuate that the dog had peed.

The days before the assembly in which I was to read my essay in front of the other classes, I rehearsed over and over again in front of my bedroom mirror. The essay was to be exactly five minutes long and I had made sure it was timed right. When my turn came, though, to ready my essay, I got on the stage and saw so many faces staring at me that I froze. Instead of speaking for the required amount of time, I kept babbling on and on and repeating things for almost double the required time. My knees and body shook so badly that I thought for sure I'd collapse right there on the stage in front of everybody. I was totally humiliated! In front of my own class, where I knew everyone, I was completely relaxed and at ease in reading my essay. But in front of strangers, it was different. Because of that one bad experience back in Grade 9, to this day I still have a hard time speaking in front of an audience.

Another time in Home Ec. class, I was assigned to iron the teacher's white bed sheets. The teacher used to bring her ironing from home for the students to do in class. I was told to drop the hanging end of the sheet in a clothes basket, so as not to let it touch the dirty floor. Something or someone distracted me though while I was ironing. When I looked away for a second or two, someone ran off with my clothes basket.

I went to retrieve the basket and, when I did, I left the hot iron sitting on the sheet. In those days, an iron had no temperature control, it just got hotter and hotter until you had to pull the plug out when it got too hot. Well, by the time I got back to the bedsheet, it had a nice, black silhouette of the iron engraved on it! Needless to say, when I tried to explain to the teacher, she was furious. And I was never assigned to do her ironing again! That incident, though, did not deter me from liking Home Ec. I loved the cooking assignments and especially the sewing.

My best friend in high school was Joan F. We met in gym class and hit it off immediately. In those days, we had to wear a one-piece navy blue outfit for gym. It consisted of baggy shorts covered over by a pleated skirt. The top of the outfit was framed by a white wing collar.

We got the bright idea one day to write our nicknames on the back of our outfits with a white marking pen. Joan decided she liked "Scotty" for a nickname and I chose "Kitty." Before long, everyone knew us as just Scotty and Kitty. Many of the students, except those from our own class, never knew our real names.

Across the street from KCI was a restaurant where the students would congregate after school for a Coke and smoke. Joan and I went there often. I didn't smoke, so I would just have a Coke. But one day Joan offered me a long, thin cigarette and told me, "Just try it. Just take a deep breath in." At first I thought she was smoking marijuana and I refused, but she laughed and said it was an American cigarette. So, stupidly, I took a long, deep drag from the cigarette and could feel my head reeling. I took a few more drags... By the time I caught my bus to go home, I was sicker than a dog.

When I arrived home an hour later, my head was still reeling. I told Mom I was sick, but didn't tell her I had been smoking. She waited on me hand and foot that night, thinking, I guess, that I was coming down with the flu or something. As sick as I was though, I tried it again the next time, and the next, until I was hooked. Back then, nothing was ever mentioned about the connection between smoking and lung cancer. I honestly don't think I would have ever started smoking if I had known about its possible side effects.

Many times after that, whenever gym class was held outdoors at the back of the school, Joan and I would sneak down the side of the hill and have a cigarette while the rest of the class was at the top of the hill playing volleyball or some other sport. When the teacher blew her whistler indicating the period was finished, Joan and I would run like hell up the hill and join the rest of the class.

One beautiful, warm morning in June the following year, Joan and I decided during our first class that it was too nice a day to be in school and thought we'd take the rest of the day off and go swimming out to Forler's gravel pit. The only problem was, we didn't have our bathing suits. So first we went to her house, which wasn't far from school, and picked up her suit. Then we had to take two buses to my house to get my suit. Just when we were ready to leave for the gravel pit, the phone rang. Not thinking, I answered it. When I heard the principal on the line asking if Beverly was there, I panicked. I said, "Yes, I'm here, and so is Joan, and we're coming back to class right away!" By the time we got back to school, the day was almost over anyway, but we got a week's detention for skipping school and had to write, "I will not skip school" about a thousand times. (I can't remember exactly how many, but it was a lot!)

Another time, Joan bleached her hair. Always having a beautiful, deep shade of chestnut brown hair, she came to school one day looking absolutely fantastic as a blond. In those days, hair colouring wasn't available in the stores as it is today, not that Joan and I were aware of anyway. "All you have to do," Joan said when I queried her on the subject, "is to mix peroxide and ammonia together and put it on your hair." So, of course, I rushed out that same day and bought some peroxide and ammonia to try and do the same.

When I got home that day, I told Mom what Joan had done. She said, "Well, don't you ever try anything stupid like that." What I didn't tell her was that I had already bought the stuff to do mine. That night I mixed the peroxide and ammonia together like Joan had told me to do (or so I thought) and put it on my hair. Within a few minutes, I thought my head was on fire. I took pillows and held them around my head to keep myself from screaming; I thought the solution would eat my scalp off!

When I look back now, I can't help but think what a stupid thing to do, to mix two chemicals like ammonia and peroxide together. It's a miracle I still had hair left after that. (That's probably why it's so thin today.) When I appeared at the breakfast table the next morning looking like Marilyn Monroe – well, almost – my parents freaked out, but eventually they got over it. I can't help but wonder what parents' emotions are today when their kids come home with purple or green or orange hair, as many kids do nowadays. Or worse, with earrings stuck through their navels, tongue, eyebrows, or – ye gads – their nipples.

The following weekend, Joan and I decided to give ourselves a perm, which is definitely a no-no after bleaching one's hair. (We were so naïve back then though, we didn't know that.) Joan was the first to take her hair out of the curlers after the perm and her hair came out in gobs. I was afraid to take mine out then. When I did, it did the same. I had a date that Saturday night with Rusty E., so when he came to pick me up, I wore a bandana around my head to cover up my hair. Eventually, our hair grew back. By this time, Joan and I were aware of hair dyes on the market and we used them. The myth though that "blondes have more fun" IS true – we definitely DID have more fun as blondes.

Eventually, Joan and I heard about the dances being held out at Bridgeport Casino every Friday and Saturday night with a live country band, so one day we decided to attend. Every Friday night thereafter, we would take the bus out to Bridgeport to the dance, but I can't remember us ever taking the bus home. We always seemed to have a date to bring us back. We sure had a lot of fun at those dances and met a lot of cute guys too. I still dated Rusty occasionally, but now I was dating others too. Fun, fun! In June, 1952, with school soon coming to an end for the summer months, all Joan and I talked about was getting a job and making some money.

20

My First Job

Before school ended for the summer in June, 1952, Joan and I saw an ad in the paper advertising for students to work at a fruit farm in Vineland, picking fruit. The ad stated that they would supply meals, lodging, and transportation. Joan and I read the ad and decided to apply. The thought of having our own money and being free to do whatever we wanted on weekends, without parental supervision, seemed a great way to spend the summer months. We sent in our application and, before long, we received notice that we were hired. A bus would pick us up at a given time to take us there, sometime in July. We were both very excited.

Then, a few days later, Joan and I decided to apply for a job at the Dominion Electrohome in Kitchener, as we had heard the pay was good there and that they might be hiring. We had to fill out an application form they provided and take a finger dexterity test to see how fast we were with our hands. After the tests were done, the foreman called us into his office and told us we did well on our tests and that we could start as soon as school was out. This job, Joan and I both knew, would pay much better than what we would get working on a fruit farm, so we accepted. (I think we started at around 90 cents an hour, which was very good pay for a female in those days.) I don't know about Joan's parents, but I'm sure my parents were relieved when I told them I wasn't going to Vineland after all.

Our first day on the job, Andy M., our foreman assigned us a position on an assembly line wiring resistors and condensors into a radio chassis. About fifteen other women were also on the assembly line, each having her own part of the radio to assemble. A few of the women also did some soldering and a few at the end of the line were inspectors.

I remember how excited I was with my first pay cheque. I splurged and bought an expensive, long-sleeved lime green, nylon blouse with a stand-up pleated collar and a black taffeta dirndl skirt with four-inch wide waistband that came to a point under my "boobs," which I thought accentuated my 24-inch waist very nicely. When I told Mom how much it cost, she almost had a fit. She said if I was going to spend money so foolishly, then I would have to pay board, although I never did.

My boss, Andy, was a short, chubby, middle-aged, dark-haired Scotsman with a great sense of humour, and a great guy to work for. In the two years that I worked at the Electrohome, I never found anything bad to say about Andy. One time, I remember though, he called me into his office and told me he was taking me off the radio line. Thinking that I was being canned, I started to cry and mumbled to Andy that I was doing my best. Realizing what I was thinking, he said, "Well, I'm not firing you, I'm promoting you to the TV line."

Another time, when I mentioned to him I was getting married (and only 15 years old), he again called me into his office and told me to think it over first, saying that after 20 years I would regret it. I was irritated by his remark and nastily replied, "Well, if I still know you then, Andy, I'll let you know if I do," and stormed out of his office. Looking back, I realize now that he was just trying to give me some good fatherly advice.

I thoroughly enjoyed my job at the Electrohome. Although we had to work hard and fast on the assembly line – we had a quota to fill every day – we also had a lot of laughs. I was only 14 when I started working. (Joan and I had lied about our age, saying we were 16.) But I seemed to age fast after that. Working with women 18-24 years of age, my thinking changed. I dressed differently and wore high heels. I wore more makeup, I guess, than I should have. And some days after work, some of us girls would head to the bar for a few beers. No one ever questioned my age back then, even though the legal drinking age was 19. (The only time I was ever asked my age at a bar was when I was in the Wellesley Hotel once with my husband, and after I had three kids!)

Every Friday after work, Joan and I would head downtown and get our hair done for the Friday night dance at Bridgeport Casino. In those days, the hairdresser washed and then set your hair in bobby pins, by curling the hair around her finger and then shoving a bobbypin through to hold it. A very tedious job compared to today's hairdressers. And I remember we always paid an extra 25 cents for a Breck shampoo. Why? Maybe it smelled better – who knows? I sure don't find anything special about Breck shampoo today.

A few weeks after I started at the Electrohome, another girl started named Gertie Q. Andy placed her across from me on the assembly line, so naturally we got to talking. When I asked her where she was from, she said Linwood. Being Rusty was also from there, I asked her if she knew him. She looked surprised at my question and exclaimed, "Why, I'm dating him!" I was as surprised as she was because I was also dating him occasionally through the week.

That summer went fast, what with working all week and going to dances or swimming or whatever on the weekends. My dates with Rusty gradually faded out, too. I was meeting other guys now and dating them. In August of that year, I met my husband to be, but that's another story for the next chapter.

When September finally rolled around, I was supposed to go back to school. You had to be sixteen to get a work permit back then, and I was only fourteen. I tried to get one, but couldn't. I had to tell Andy that I had lied about my age and could no longer continue working. I thought he'd really be mad that I had lied, but instead he said he would see what he could do for me. He made a few phone calls to someone and was told I could apply for a permit again on my fifteenth birthday which was that October but, until then, I had to go back to school.

So for two months I attended school – and hated it! I had no incentive to do any homework or studying, knowing that as soon as my birthday rolled around, I would be going back to work anyway. I spent a lot of those next few weeks either skipping classes or hanging out in the washroom having a smoke. I had no intention of buying any books either for only two months.

Finally, my birthday came, and I was back on the assembly line with my buddies, and loving every minute of it.

21

Meeting My Husband-To-Be

It was in August, 1952, that I met my husband to be. Joan and I were strolling down King Street in Kitchener one warm, sunny afternoon when we ran into Leonard G. and another guy, which I'll name Ron for reading purposes because I can't remember his real name. We got talking with them and soon they asked us if we wanted to accompany them to a garden party at the Catholic Church in St. Clements. Ron owned a red convertible, and whether it was this attraction or not that prompted us to go with them, I don't know, but we said yes. I jumped in the back with Leonard, Joan in the front with Ron. With our hair blowing in the wind, off we drove to St. Clements.

After arriving at the garden party, Ron informed Joan that he had a confession to make. He was going steady with a girl who he was supposed to pick up after she had finished work that day. He said he had to leave, but would be back as soon as he took her home.

Well, it wasn't too long after Ron left that Lorne Vollmer (my now husband) came on the scene. Lorne knew Leonard, my date, and he, Leonard, Joan and I started a conversation. One thing led to another and soon Lorne and Joan, Len and me, became a foursome. Ron, in the meantime, never did show up. Eventually, Lorne wound up taking Joan home, and I went home with Leonard.

While at work on Monday morning, I found out from Joan that she gave Lorne a bloody nose that night. Did he get fresh? I never did find out. Lorne tells me now that they were just horsing around, but who knows? Joan did confess though, that she thought Lorne was pretty nice stuff.

The following week, Joan was grounded for staying out so late, so I went to the dance at Bridgeport Casino with some other friends when Lorne came on the scene again. He asked for a dance and I accepted. Before the evening ended, he asked to take me home. From then on, we dated pretty steady. Maybe I should have felt guilty for going out with Lorne when Joan had gone out with him first but, at the time, I didn't really think much about it because Joan, it seemed, always had a string of guys wanting to date her.

Joan eventually married Jack A. and they went on to have five children together before he died of throat cancer.

Back to 1952…In October of that year, Lorne and I broke up, for reasons unknown now, and I started dating Franklin B., a guy in the air force that I met at Bridgeport Casino. We dated occasionally for three months, but in the meantime, my heart was pining for Lorne. At Christmas, I can remember buying the record *Blue Christmas* and playing it over and over. I must have driven my parents nuts.

I rang in the new year with Frank, who invited me to a house party at his place while his parents were out of town on holiday. In January, Lorne and I got back together again. In February, we got engaged. On a very cold Saturday morning, we went to a jewellery store in Kitchener on King Street and purchased a ring. On the way back to the car that day, I never wore any gloves because I was so proud of my ring and wanted to show it off to anyone who might notice. (But no one did!)

When we arrived at my house, I flashed the ring at my parents. They never really said too much, other than congratulating us, as they truly liked Lorne. But I think too, it was because when they'd become engaged, they had so much hassle from their own parents that they didn't want a repeat of their own engagement. My mother, being Catholic, was raised in a strict Catholic home, and my dad, being Protestant, was raised in a strict Protestant home. My mother's father refused to even go to their wedding. My dad's family was also very upset about the marriage, so much so that my mom and dad eventually got married in the parsonage of Zion's Evangelical Church in Kitchener with only their attendants present.

Lorne and I set the wedding date for June 13 of that year, 1953. We agreed that I would turn Catholic. Therefore, I would have to take instructions before taking my vows. As I was only 15, I had to have parental consent to get married. If my parents thought I was too young to get married, they never said so. They thought a lot of Lorne and so agreed to the marriage. We would get married in St. Mary's RC Church with Father Durand officiating.

A week before the wedding, Lorne's sister, Betty, and I attended a Beisinger wedding at Hesson church. My main reason for going was to watch the proceedings and see what I would have to do the following week when Lorne and I took our turn. As I walked into the church, I was surprised to see Rusty as one of the attendants. We merely said hi to each other. But the following week, Rusty came to the house to see if I'd go out with him. I wasn't home at the time and my Dad came out and told Rusty, "Get the hell out. She's getting married next week!" Mom dropped that tidbit of information to me years later.

2 2

A Bit About Lorne

From the first time I set eyes on Lorne, I was attracted to him. He was lean and muscular, with a country-boy smile and tan. He was the kind of guy you're not embarrassed to take home to meet Mom and Dad.

He was the fifth of ten children born to Bill and Anne Vollmer. He grew up on an 85-acre farm about ten miles east of Listowel, Ontario, on what was then Highway 86, now Line 86.

With ten children in the family, times were tough and Lorne knew what work was from an early age. He had chores to do each morning in the barn before going to school. He helped feed the calves, fork hay and straw into the cow feeders, and also milked cows. As he told me, "One day all the men were away and my mother needed milk for the baby, so she sent me to the barn to try and milk a cow." He successfully managed to fill the pail a couple of inches and took it to the house. From then on, it was his job to milk the cow each morning. After school, there were still more chores to do in the barn. As Lorne got older, he had three or four cows to milk each morning before going to school.

The summers were even busier. There was always ploughing, seeding, haying, stooking grain or gardening to be done. Sometimes during summer, Lorne worked for Eddy L. cleaning cattle pens, for which he received the big sum of $1.00 a day. Summer holidays were unheard of – too much farm work to be done, no time to waste.

Until Lorne was 14, their house had no electricity, so homework was done around a coal oil lamp. The house was heated by a coal furnace, but a wood stove in the kitchen provided a little extra warmth during the harsh winters.

Back then, the families didn't have cars. A horse and buggy was their only means of travel, so a trip to the store wasn't too frequent. When they did go, they made sure they got everything they needed in one trip.

Lorne received his education at Tralee USS (Union School Section) No. 10 Mornington School. He walked to school every day, a distance of about two miles, although sometimes if the weather was really bad during the winter months, his Dad would take the children by sleigh. One teacher taught all eight grades. When Lorne started Grade 1, the classroom was filled to capacity, but when he finished Grade 8, there were only 18 pupils. His favourite teacher was Eleanor Fallis. He attended Listowel Secondary School for a couple months, but then quit to help his father on the farm.

Sunday was a day of rest. Sunday morning the family went to church and, in the afternoon, they had a bit of free time, usually spent playing cards, if they could find a deck. Often though, the decks were so worn out that they would take cornstarch and spread the cards around in it so they wouldn't stick together. Sometimes during the winter, the kids would go skating in the field, wherever they could find some ice. Sometimes they would build a rink and would sneak water from the well to flood it, but there was hell to pay later if Mom or Dad saw them taking water from the well.

Lorne's younger brother, Edgar, was born with Down's syndrome. In those days he was referred to as a "blue baby." He weighed only two pounds, two ounces at birth, and was born at home, as were all the children. It was a miracle that he even survived, but he did.

Although Edgar had a very limited vocabulary, I can remember one Easter when Lorne told him the Easter bunny had come. Edgar mumbled a bit, looked around the room and clearly questioned, "Where the 'ell did he go?"

Edgar was also very neat and tidy. He had his toys in the dresser arranged just so and would get furious if one of his younger nieces or nephews took something out and messed things up. In later years when he would come to our farm, he would move the chairs around in the kitchen to his own liking and straighten out the fringe on the mats. Edgar also hated flies and, if he saw one – what farm doesn't have flies? – he would quickly grab the fly swatter. I would cringe every time because when Edgar hit a fly, he was a real power house. My wallpaper suffered for that.

Edgar attended school for a few months, but eventually was taken out as he wasn't learning anything. The teacher didn't have the time to devote to one child and also didn't have the capabilities to deal with a retarded one. But Edgar had one good quality that a lot of people could use – he was lovable. When you went for a visit, Edgar was always ready to give you a hug or shake your hand. When he was born, the doctors predicted he would only live to his teens, but today, as I write this, he is 62 and lives in a group home in Erbsville. The doctors blamed Edgar's Down syndrome on Lorne's mother having a child so late in life, but a year later she had another child who did not have Down's.

Lorne left home at 16 and sent to live with his brothers, Carl and Sheldon, in Petersburg, Ontario. While there, in order to help pay his board, he helped out at the garage his brothers owned, pumping gas, driving the tow truck, etc., whatever needed doing.

One weekend, not too long after Lorne was there, Carl took him to a show in Kitchener. On the way home, Lorne complained he was sick, so Carl drove him to a doctor in New Hamburg who diagnosed appendicitis. Carl then drove Lorne back to Kitchener where he was admitted to St. Mary's Hospital and operated on the next day. While in the hospital, he took double pneumonia, so his stay there was much longer than expected.

On his return to Petersburg, Lorne helped out at the Blue Moon Hotel, which was across the street from the garage. He washed dishes as he couldn't do much else after his operation. After his strength returned, he did other odd jobs, such as lugging beer cases up from the basement or sweeping floors at the hotel, while at the same time helping out in the garage whenever he could in order to help pay his board.

In 1949, Elmer G., an acquaintance of Lorne's who worked at the Canadian Brass in Galt (now Cambridge), told Lorne they were hiring, so Lorne applied and was hired to work in the machine shop. His starting wage was $1 an hour, pretty good wages at the time. Lorne worked there until we married in June, 1953.

23

The Wedding Day

Our wedding took place June 13, 1953. The wedding announcement in the *K-W Record* read as follows:

KINGSDALE BRIDE IS WED AT HESSON

HESSON – Bouquets of spring flowers decorated St. Mary's RC Church, Hesson, Saturday when Rev. R. Durand, Wingham, performed the wedding ceremony uniting Miss Beverly Janet Beilstein, only daughter of Mr. and Mrs. Norman Beilstein of Kingsdale, to Mr. Lawrence William Vollmer, son of Mr. and Mrs. William Vollmer, RR 3, Listowel.

CHURCH CHOIR SINGS

Mrs. Carl Linesman and the church choir sang at the ceremony. The bride, given in marriage by her father, was lovely in a gown of drift white nylon net and Chantilly lace tissue taffeta designed with strapless lace bodice and bouffant skirt of net. Her veil of illusion net fell from a pleated net headdress. She carried red roses and white carnations.

TWO ATTENDANTS

The bridegroom's sister-in-law, Mrs. Elgin Vollmer, RR3, Listowel, wore a gown of yellow net over taffeta. The bodice was in a flange style and the skirt fell in soft gathering from a snuggly fitted waist. She wore a yellow bolero, braided headdress and carried yellow carnations and mauve sweet peas.

The bridesmaid, Mrs. George Graff, Millbank, sister of the bridegroom, wore a gown of ice blue satin styled with a low, square neckline, satin bodice with a satin bolero and nylon net overskirt. Her braided headdress matched her gown, and she carried a bouquet of pink carnations with white sweet peas.

Miss Donna Blanche Dobson of Ethel, niece of the bridegroom, was flower girl in a dainty frock of romance pink nylon net over satin, with braided headdress. She carried a miniature bouquet of pink and white sweet peas with pink streamers.

Attending the bridegroom were his brother, Mr. Elgin Vollmer of RR3 Listowel, and brother-in-law, Mr. George Graff of Millbank. The ushers were Mr. Gordon Stemmler of Waterloo and Mr. John Basler, Jr., of RR3, Listowel.

A reception followed the ceremony at the home of the bridegroom's parents.

Mrs. Norman Beilstein received in a gown of ice blue with black accessories and corsage of red roses.

150 ATTEND RECEPTION

The bridegroom's mother assisted in a gown of ice blue with white accessories and corsage of red roses. Dinner and supper were served for 70 guests.

About 150 friends of the bride and bridegroom gathered in the evening at Tralee School for a reception.

Music for dancing was supplied by Foell's Orchestra of Glen Allan. For a trip north, the bride wore a sky blue dress, a yellow short coat, and white accessories.

Mr. and Mrs. Lorne Vollmer will reside at RR3, Listowel.

***

My parents wanted to have the wedding in Kitchener, but we were getting married in Hesson and the reception in the evening was at Tralee School, and most of the guests were from that area, so it was decided to have the meals at Lorne's home.

The waitresses who helped out at the meals were from the neighbourhood and included Jackelyn Basler, Eileen Basler, Mary Ann Kraemer, Peggy Kraemer, and Ester Stemmler

I have to say here that Lorne's mother put an extreme amount of hard work into our wedding. Besides preparing the two meals for 70-plus people, she also made and decorated the wedding cake. She also arranged for girls in the neighbourhood to work as waitresses, besides all the work she had of cleaning the house before and after the wedding. All that, only four months after her own daughter's marriage. Looking back now, I wonder how she ever did it – she truly was a remarkable woman!

On the morning of the wedding, my cousin, Harold, came to take pictures. He wasn't a professional photographer, but had taken many courses on photography and offered to do it. And besides, he was cheap, a big plus back then for us. In those days, pictures were mostly developed in black and white, although I do have a few with a bit of tinting in them.

Our wedding was a far cry from today's elaborate weddings, which can cost thousands. I don't know how parents can afford them. And the sad part is that many of today's marriages end in divorce within a few years' time.

Mom, Dad and I drove to Hesson the day of my wedding in Dad's 1932 Model A Ford. We first drove to the farm of Lorne's parents where the wedding party gathered before going to the church.

For our honeymoon, we drove to Midland in Lorne's 1940 Mercury and got a room there. I remember the proprietor looking at us warily, as if thinking we were just two kids shacking up for the night. When she handed Lorne the key to our room, she casually mentioned (or was she warning us) that a police officer would be staying in the room adjacent to ours. She did, however, take our picture for us the next day and was very friendly when we talked with her.

The following day, Lorne and I went to the beach, but it was too cold for swimming, so we travelled to Penetang, watched the boats come in for a while, and then drove to Midland and a tour of the Martyrs' Shrine before heading home. When we arrived back at the farm, Lorne's dad was haying, so it wasn't too long before Lorne donned some work clothes and was out pitching hay bales. It was then I realized — the honeymoon WAS over.

Although the newspaper clipping from the *K-W Record* stated that we would reside at RR3, Listowel, it wasn't true. After the wedding, I continued living at home with my parents, while working at the Electrohome in Kitchener. Lorne, meanwhile, had quit his job at the Canadian Brass in Cambridge and rented his Uncle Joe's farm for the summer. The farm was just up the road from his dad's place. Lorne continued to live with his parents, while looking after the chickens and a few cattle which he had purchased.

Weekends, though, and occasionally through the week, Lorne would come to Kitchener and then we'd visit friends or take in a movie or dance. Lorne and I both loved country music and, in those days, nothing was more enjoyable than going to a dance with a live country band.

That fall, Lorne went back to work at the Canadian Brass. Meanwhile, my parents put in a dormer on their Second Avenue house and added an apartment upstairs which Lorne and I eventually moved into. We lived there for about a year, until we decided we wanted to be on our own and purchased our first home at 82 Broadview Avenue in Kitchener. The timing proved to be good, as we soon discovered baby number one was on the way.

24

Our First Home

When my Uncle Jack and Aunt Effie (Dad's sister) decided to put their house at 82 Broadview Avenue in Kitchener up for sale in 1954, Lorne and I decided to purchase it. So we scraped together $2,600 for the down payment and mortgaged the rest from Leena R. Our house payments were $25 per month. In today's terms, that doesn't seem like much, but Lorne was only making around $1.50 an hour back then.

I was already familiar with the house because Uncle Jack's and Aunt Effie's children – my cousins, Jean, Jack, Merle, Leon, Phyllis and Bobby – all went to Sunnyside School, which I had attended. Phyllis and I were the same age and were in the same class. Leon was also in the same class, but was a year younger than us. (In those days, there were three grades to a classroom.) As kids, Phyllis and I played a lot together and often spent the night at each other's home.

Lorne and I moved into the house that fall, 1954, while Uncle Jack and Aunt Effie moved into a new house that they had had built for themselves, their first new home after raising six kids. Ironically, they were only in the house a few months when Aunt Effie discovered she had breast cancer. She died the following year.

When we moved, the house was in bad need of repair. The roof was worn out and the imitation brick siding needed replacing. On the back of the house was an old shanty, but a few days after we moved in, Lorne's brother, Carl, who was a very large man, came for a visit. He stood in the doorway of the shanty and said to Lorne, "You don't need this!" or something to that effect. With his arms stretched against the sides of the doorway, he pushed his arms out and the shanty fell apart. I had no regrets either, as it was a real eyesore.

The storey-and-a-half house downstairs consisted of three small rooms – a kitchen, bedroom, livingroom – with a short hall leading to the front of the house. In the hall was a cubbyhole, like a closet without a door, where we kept the refrigerator because the kitchen was too small. Steps at the front of the house led to two small bedrooms upstairs. The bathroom and furnace were in the basement. Because we heated with coal, a room in the basement served as a coal bin, and a window served as a coal chute for pouring in the coal. A friend who had visited me for the first time, after we had fixed up the place, remarked that our house looked like a "little doll house."

Out the back was an arbour covered in grape vines which produced the most delectable grapes that my dad picked to make grape wine. One year Lorne made wine, but when Dad made a habit of coming over every night to taste the wine, Lorne told him to take the wine and barrel home with him.

Beyond the arbour was a garden and a large, yellow harvest apple tree. I remember as a kid, Aunt Effie phoning my mother and telling her how she had placed a stuffed owl in the apple tree to fool the neighbours and how they all came over to have a look at the owl. I remember my mother laughing so hard while on the phone and again when she relayed the story to Dad and me.

Once we got settled in, we started renovating the place. Dad put on a new roof and new siding and laid new floors, while I painted, made ruffled curtains for the kitchen and drapes for the livingroom, and put flower beds out front.

The following year, I planted flowers in two small barrels which I purchased. I set one barrel at each corner of our lot. One day, I happened to look out the window on garbage day, just in time to see the garbage collector picking up one of the barrels and pitching it onto the garbage truck. I remember running, pregnant as can be, out of the house and down the street after the garbage truck to get my barrel back. I did manage to retrieve it without much damage, but I sure was embarrassed in the process.

On June 30 of that year, 1955, Brian Joseph was born, followed by Michael Lawrence, April 20, 1957, and Donna Marie, October 5, 1958.

Those were rough years, financially speaking, as money was tight, with only Lorne working and five mouths to feed. I learned to stretch the budget a million different ways to make Lorne's pay cheque go around. We never really thought of ourselves as poor though. Our kids were healthy and we had food to eat, even though we weren't dining on caviar and T-bone steak, so that was all that mattered. Mom and Dad helped out a lot, too, especially in the babysitting department on weekends when Lorne and I would take in a drive-in movie or go to a dance. As the kids got older, they went with us to the drive-in too, but at that point in time, they were still too young.

I can remember buying material in large quantities from Eaton's catalogue and then making clothes for the kids out of it. When you purchased a bundle of fabric, you never knew what you were getting, as each length was from a different fabric bolt. Some lengths maybe would be two or three yards long and some only one yard, never shorter though, and you never had a choice of fabric. But I always thought of it as a challenge, as well as fun, trying to decide what to make out of each piece. Back then, the unit for measuring fabric was yards; metric was still unheard of.

The fall of 1958, shortly after Donna was born, Lorne heard there was a farm for sale on Highway 86, near Listowel, just up the road from his dad. By this time, Lorne was getting sick of factory work and decided he wanted to try farming, so he quit his job at Canadian Brass, and we purchased a farm from Joe and Rita Brunen for $9,500, with a $5,000 mortgage. Brunens also purchased our house on Broadview for $7,200, although they had no intention of moving in, only purchasing it from us so they could sell the farm. They figured they would have an easier time selling a house in town than they would a farm.

I wasn't too enthusiastic about moving to the farm, as I had grown up in Kitchener and all my friends and relatives lived there, including my parents who only lived a few blocks away, but Lorne was eager to go, so I agreed. The following spring, 1959, with three kids in tow, we moved in.

25

Moving to the Farm

If I thought the house on Broadview Avenue was rough when we moved in, it was nothing compared to the 100-year-old farmhouse we were about to move into. Looking back now, I think we must have been out of our minds to buy the place, but it was all we could afford at the time.

To begin with, the house had been empty a year or two before we moved in, so the place was filthy, with spiders and dirt everywhere, and was in desperate need of repair. At the back of the house was a dilapidated old room that, at one time, had been a former owner's summer kitchen, but later had been converted into a garage. It had a dirt floor, as the original floor was torn out when they decided to make it into a garage. At the one end was a pipe sticking out of the ground, the only source of water in the house.

Except for a lilac tree at the front of the house, which was so big it eventually had to be taken down anyway, the landscaping was almost nil, with three-foot weeds and stones surrounding the place. Big pieces of broken, ugly cement slabs led to the rickety old steps at the back door.

A few weeks before we were to move in, my mom watched the kids while Lorne and I drove to the farm to start cleaning up. At the front of the house was a small sunroom (supposedly) which consisted of wall-to-wall windows which were so filthy and crawling with hideous spiders and other bugs that, to me, the thought of cleaning them seemed appalling, to say the least, since I have a terrible phobia of spiders and bugs, especially spiders.

Armed with a bucket of cold water (no hot water available), and a scrub rag and whisk, I proceeded to whisk the spiders and webs down – I didn't own a vacuum cleaner back then either – but in so doing, I became more and more depressed until I found myself in tears. I continued working and crying though, until I happened to see through my tears and the murky, filthy windows my neighbor, Dorothy D., coming across the field for a visit.

I had met Dorothy only briefly once before when Lorne and I were driving through Milverton and Lorne had seen her and her husband, Ivan, walking up the street. Lorne pulled over with the car to talk to them and introduced us. So, when I saw her coming across the field that day, I was in a state of panic. I'll never forget how humiliated I felt at that moment in my filthy clothes and tear-stained face, trying to make friendly conversation with a woman I barely knew.

The main floor of our farmhouse consisted of only two large rooms – a kitchen and livingroom. In the livingroom was a door that didn't lead anywhere, only opening into the wall. Apparently, the previous owners were going to put on an addition leading into the garage, but never did. The only good thing about that house was the beautiful hardwood floor in the livingroom which I eventually, years later, covered in wall-to-wall rug because of the work involved in cleaning it – removing the old wax, scrubbing it, applying paste wax, polishing with a floor polisher – a job that took me a complete day to do at least three times a year. The hardwood floors today are a breeze to clean compared to the hardwood floors of yesteryear.

The kitchen was huge but without cupboards, sink, or water when we moved in. The only water available came from the tap protruding from the ground in the old rickety garage at the back of the house. For the first while after we moved in, every time I needed water for cooking, cleaning, washing dishes and clothes, rinsing diapers or whatever, I had to run out the back with a pail. If I wanted hot water, then I had to first heat it on the stove. One of the first jobs Lorne did in the house was to hook up water for the kitchen, install a sink and cupboards (our brother-in-law, Gord S., built them).

There was no bathroom in the house either, which meant no shower or toilet. We had to use a pail for over a year before the toilet was installed. When the pail was full, I had to take it out the back to the edge of the lot and dump it. It was a job I despised every time. Then I had the ugly job of cleaning the pail. Yuck! Plus, the diapers from two children had to be rinsed in a pail and dumped outside.

Many times during that first year, Lorne would drive me and the kids to my mother's on a Friday night and we'd stay until Sunday when Dad would drive us home again. While at Mom's we would all have a bath. Let me tell you, there is absolutely no better feeling in this world than to be able to relax in a nice hot bath, especially when you don't have a tub at home. That old saying, "You don't appreciate something until you don't have it" is so true.

That first winter we darn near froze to death as there was no insulation anywhere in the house and there were no furnace pipes going upstairs. Once you got undressed, you didn't waste time getting into bed. The first winter we were on the farm, Lorne's mother gave me a patchwork tie quilt that she had made out of heavy pants fabric. It was nothing fancy, and it weighed a ton, but it sure helped to keep me warm on many a cold winter's night. I had that quilt for many years and eventually it came to town with us. But since I have no use for it now in our cozy warm house, I gave it to my daughter, Charin. I hope she treasures it as much as I did.

We never had a telephone for the first six or seven years on the farm because we couldn't afford one. The few times that we needed to phone, we would go across the field to our neighbours, Dorothy and Ivan, and use their phone. Their house, like ours, was also freezing in winter. The wind blew in every crack and cranny. When I went over there in the winter, Dorothy always had quilts hanging over the wainscoting in the kitchen to keep the wind from blowing in.

Once, when I went over to use their phone on an extremely cold winter's day, Ivan (unbeknownst to me) had just come downstairs in the nude after having taken a shower. When he heard me coming in the livingroom to use the phone, he dashed behind the first hiding place he could think of – behind the door. As I talked away to Mom on the telephone, Ivan was literally freezing to death behind the door. Years later, after I got to know Dorothy and Ivan better, they told me about that incident. To this day, Lorne and I still laugh about it.

Upstairs in our house were three bedrooms – one large and two small ones – and each covered in at least three layers of wallpaper which took me a year to remove, in what little spare time I had with three little children to care for.

A railing went along the stairs from the livingroom and along the hall in the upstairs. At the end of the hall was a door which again didn't lead anywhere except outside – with no landing or porch of any kind. It was a long drop from the door to the ground so, needless to say, we kept that door locked. Years later, we installed a window there.

When Dad visited the farm for the first time and went upstairs, the first thing he did was rush out and buy a couple sheets of plywood to cover up the railing, fearing one of the kids might fall through the rungs. He also thought a small pump house down by the barn was an outhouse.

The basement of the house resembled a dwelling our ancestors may have lived in years ago, with low ceilings and walls consisting of rocks with mortar in between. Cubbyholes cut in the rocks were used for storing things. Every time I think of that basement, I can't help but think of that kid's TV show called *The Flintstones*. They lived in a stone house that resembled our basement.

After we moved in, Lorne got a job working at McKee Brothers in Elmira, working on farm machinery. We only had about eight cattle that first year and a few hens. We couldn't afford much else. Every cent we had either went into repairing something on the house or barn.

Lorne did, however, plant some grain and took in hay. He and his dad and brother Elgin worked together sharing equipment, so there was a little time for relaxing after work. As soon as Lorne got home from work and had supper, he was either heading out to the barn to fix something or up to his dad's or Elgin's to work again up there. On rainy days when the men couldn't work outside, there was always something to fix in the house or in the barn.

My work was endless, too. There was always something to be done, what with washing, ironing, cleaning, sewing for the kids and myself, painting and wallpapering. Washday was every other day, which meant lugging the old washing machine out of the corner to the kitchen sink and filling it with water. Then I had to fill the galvanized tub for rinsing the clothes. After the clothes were washed, they had to be put through the wringer and into the rinse water, then rinsed, and again through the wringer into the basket. Nothing was more irritating than when the clothes would go around the wringer and I'd have to stop and untangle them. I always had to fill the washing machine three times – once each for whites, coloured clothes, and diapers. It would take a whole morning just to do the wash. I didn't own a clothes dryer back then, so the wash had to be hung out, winter or summer.

We somehow managed to survive that first year though and, as rough as things were, we had good times, too. Many a Saturday night in the winter, we spent at one of the neighbours, or they with us, for a game of cards and a lot of laughs. Sometimes, we'd load the kids up and visit Lorne's mom and dad for the evening. Club 86 was just up the road from us and held dances there on a monthly basis, so Mom and Dad would sometimes come up and watch the kids while we went dancing.

Initially, I dreaded having to move to the farm but, gradually, I began to like farm life.

26

More On The Way

The next few years went by fairly quickly. Lorne continued to work at McKee Brothers for about a year and a half until they folded up and went broke after the John Diefenbaker government's policies caused the farmers to get into such financial difficulties that they couldn't afford to buy machinery.

After being unemployed for about four or five months, Lorne got a job working for a construction company in Moorefield, driving a truck that had poor steering and brakes. He only worked there for about six weeks and, after nearly getting killed a couple of times, he quit because he felt the truck wasn't safe. Then, he went on unemployment again, but had to put in eight weeks waiting time, then wait another two weeks before collecting any money. When the unemployment cheque finally came through, it only amounted to a measly $72.

In January, 1961, we welcomed another addition to our family – William (Bill) John Vollmer. Brian also started school that fall.

Times were really tough that year with Lorne still out of work. He was collecting unemployment, but that didn't go too far with a family of six to feed. Occasionally, he would work for his brother-in-law, George G., who had a small body shop in Hesson fixing cars, farm machinery, garden tractors, etc. But George couldn't pay Lorne very much either, as he had a large family of nine to feed, including himself.

Lorne bought ten cattle from Elwood O. that year for $75 each on a note. Lorne eventually managed to pay off the note by cashing in a pension fund he had built up while working at the Canadian Brass factory in Galt. Later that year, Elwood got sick and was admitted to hospital. Elwood's mother, who lived with him, asked Lorne if he would do the chores for Elwood while he was in hospital, so Lorne agreed to do them. But eventually Elwood died and Lorne had to wait until the estate was settled before he got paid, which amounted to $70. Nearly all of Ellwood's estate was left to the St. Joseph's Church in Listowel to pay off the church's mortgage.

As Christmas approached that year, I worried constantly about how we would be able to afford gifts for the children because, as the saying goes, we were poor as church mice. But fortunately, Campbell Soup opened a plant in Listowel that year. Lorne quickly applied for a maintenance position, fixing machinery, and was hired a few months before Christmas. It was like a gift from heaven! His starting wage was $1.20 an hour, working up to $1.69 an hour after three months. Nearly all of his first pay cheque went to buy tools for the job. He worked there for nearly ten years.

In August, 1963, we welcomed yet another addition to our family – Sharon Ann – born the Monday after the August civic holiday weekend. Our family doctor had just gotten back from his cottage when he got the call from the hospital that one of his patients was in labour. I remember him rushing into the room, still sprouting his weekend beard, and asking, "Was that you screaming?" I looked at him and said, "No." Apparently another patient of his was also in labour at the same time and she was down the hall screaming, so she got top priority of the delivery room. Thank God Sharon waited her turn.

(The spelling of Sharon's name is now Charin. She had it legally changed when she was older.)

As much as I loved having children – I would have had ten if it wasn't for all the work involved – after Sharon was born, Lorne and I decided our family was complete, so I had a tubal ligation while I was still in the hospital. If I had to do it over again though, I wouldn't have had it done. To begin with, when a woman has a tubal ligation, she has a three-inch vertical scar running down from her navel, besides the pain from the operation itself. It is so much simpler for the man to get sterilized. If the woman has to go through the labour, then the man should at least be the one who gets sterilized.

It wasn't until Sharon was around seven or eight years old that I got my first washer and dryer. I was ecstatic! No more having to drag the washing machine from the far end of the kitchen to the sink, or having to fill the machine and rinse tub two or three times with fresh water or having to hangout the wash in the winter. And no more frozen fingers or aching back! Wow!

27

Bits About The Children

Looking back to the time when my children were young, certain things come to mind, so I thought I would write about a few of them, starting with Brian.

I bought Brian his first snowsuit when he was only six months old, a yellow velvet one with long bunny ears. Every day in the winter, I'd bundle him in it and put him out in his buggy on the front porch of our Broadview Avenue home for a half hour of fresh air. He was a real sweety in that suit. Of course, I had to go and check on him every few minutes or so.

Brian started school in September, 1961, the same year Bill was born. By this time, we were living on the farm. As there were no school buses back then, Brian had to walk to Hesson school a distance of approximately 1.5 miles. The first day of school, Brian came home at recess. He thought school was over for the day. As we didn't yet have a phone and I still hadn't learned to drive, I had no way of letting the teacher know where Brian was. It wasn't too long before Florence M., the principal at the time, came to the house wondering if Brian was there. She sure was relieved when I told her he had come home at recess.

During the winter, we paid Fred S. a few bucks to pick Brian up and bring him home. Fred said to Lorne one day, "I don't know why I drive

Brian to school and home because, as soon as he gets out of the car, he rolls around in the snow so much, he's soaked by the time he gets in the school or back in the house."

Another time when Lorne and I and the kids were out for a Sunday drive, just out of the blue, Brian asked, "Daddy, where do babies come from?" My quick-thinking spouse calmly told him that they had to be ordered from the Eaton's catalogue. Brian accepted that answer at the time, but I was furious with Lorne for giving him such an evasive answer. Secretly, though, I was happy that Brian had asked Lorne and not me that question. I don't know what my response would have been.

Mike started school in September, 1963, when Sharon was only a month old. By the time he started, though, there were school buses to take the children to and from school, a great relief to me as I always worried about the children walking along the highway in the winter. Winters back then were a lot worse than they are today. Many times the snow banks were almost as high as the telephone wires.

One time during the summer, Lorne and I went into town to do our grocery shopping, taking Mike, who was around four at the time. As we were approaching the A&P store on Main Street, Mike looked up at the moon and asked, "Daddy, how many moons are there?" Lorne replied, "Just one." Mike quickly retorted, "No, Daddy, you're wrong. When we left home, there was one up above the barn and now," he pointed to the sky, "there's another one up there." I always have to laugh when I think of that.

Another time, when the kids were older, we had an overabundance of pumpkins. Lorne wouldn't let me put out a "Pumpkins For Sale" sign so, when he was out of sight one day, I loaded the trunk of the car with pumpkins to take into town to sell. (By this time, I had a driver's license.) I asked the kids who would go with me door to door to try and sell them. Mike, who was around ten, was the only one who volunteered. With the four youngest children in the car, away we went to town to unload our pumpkins.

When we arrived in town though, Mike chickened out and refused to go with me to the houses. So while I went to the first house, the kids sat in the car watching me out the car window. Well, the woman in the house didn't want any pumpkins, so I went next door and the woman there bought a pumpkin. When the kids saw me handing her a pumpkin, Mike stuck his head out the car window, yelling, "Yeah for Mom. Yeah for Mom!" I was so embarrassed.

I went to a few more homes, but couldn't make a sale. I wound up going to the A&P grocery store and asking the Manager if he wanted to buy any pumpkins. He bought the whole load, so we all went home happy that day and a few dollars richer.

When Donna was around 8 or 9 years old, she made her first communion. I sewed her a beautiful white dress for the occasion. After church, I left the kids on their own while I went into the house to prepare dinner. Minutes later, I happened to look out the window to see Donna – still wearing her white communion dress – whizzing by the window in a cloud of dust on the go-cart the boys had made and the boys behind it pushing her.

Another time, I happened to go outside for something just in time to see Donna lying on top of the gas barrel with her nose in the gas spout. I asked her what she was doing and she said, "I get a funny feeling, Mommy, when I put my nose in here." I didn't waste time getting her down from there! It's a wonder the fumes didn't kill her.

Donna loved to read, as did the rest of the children, but Donna always amazed me the way she could stick with a book for so long without putting it down (and without getting a headache).

Donna's best friend was Shelley D., who lived next door. They got along great and were always playing together. Around the time they were seven or eight, Barbie dolls came on the market. When they first appeared on toy store shelves, with their tiny waists and big boobs, Shelley's mother, Dorothy, remarked that no daughter of hers would ever be allowed to play with Barbies as they were nothing but "sex dolls." Eventually, Donna and Shelley both acquired Barbie dolls and they spent countless hours playing with them for many years.

Bill was the acrobat in the family. He liked to climb trees, hang upside down, swinging with his knees draped over the branch, especially when I was in view, anything to scare the hell out of me. The more I hollered for him to come down, the higher he'd climb or the more he'd swing, just to irritate me.

One time, I decided to paint the outside windows on the second level of our house. I got Lorne to prop the extension ladder up against the window for me before he went to work in the morning. I had taken the entire window out from inside the house earlier, with the intention of having something to hang onto while I painted the outside trim.

I am deathly afraid of heights and could not make it to the top of that ladder no matter how many times I tried. I'd get half way up, get scared, and have to come back down again. After several tries, I finally gave up. Later, while I was preparing supper, Bill arrived home from school, coming in the kitchen from the livingroom. When I asked him how he got in, he nonchalantly replied, "Through the upstairs window." Here I was, terrified of going up the ladder and Bill, only seven years old, had climbed up without any reservations about it.

Charin was the tomboy in the family. She was always thinking up excuses to go to the barn after supper, rather than help me with the dishes. Charin loved all animals, especially dogs and horses. When she was around ten, Lorne bought her a pony. She didn't have it very long though, when we discovered Charin had a hernia and needed an operation. I also had a hernia in the very same spot, so it was decided I would have mine operated on first, then Charin. The day I got out of the hospital, I could hardly move because I was in so much pain. When Charin got out of the hospital, the first thing she did was run to the barn, get on her pony, and take off. (To my amazement.)

Before Charin was old enough to go to school, she played with Bobby D. a lot. In the winter, they would take turns playing at each other's house. It always gave Dorothy and me a bit of a break when they played at the other's house. One day Dorothy phoned and said, "Bev, you'd better get over here right away. Bobby and Charin were playing hairdresser, and Bobby just cut Charin's hair." What a mess it was...imagine the cut a four-year-old would give!

Another time when Charin and Bobby were colouring, I gave them a dull paring knife to sharpen their crayons. When I was out of sight, one of them (I never did find out which) ran the knife down the centre of my beautiful rubber plant and killed it. I was really upset, as rubber plants are very slow growing.

Once when Brian was about five years old, I sent him to the barn to collect the chicken eggs and he put them in the baby stroller. By the time he got to the house, there was only one egg left as the rest had rolled through the leg holes of the stroller. So Brian picked up the last egg and pitched it.

Another time, Mike bought fire crackers when he was told he couldn't. The firecrackers caught fire in his pockets and burned his legs. And once, when my dad lay down for a Sunday snooze, Mike went into the room, saw Dad's cigarettes and lighter lying on the night table, then grabbed the lighter and hid under the bed. Eventually, my dad woke up because he smelled smoke. He hollered downstairs to me and asked if I was burning something in the kitchen. When I said, "No," he checked under the bed and found the fringe of the chenille bedspread smouldering. Mike had tried to light it. Now that could have been a real disaster!

Yes, there are probably many more stories I could write about my children, but I would have to probe deeply into my brain to remember them all. Over the years, many things are forgotten, but there are others neatly tucked away in my memory, only to occasionally pop out now and then.

28

My Friends

I met Nancy shortly after moving to the farm. She was married to Lorne's cousin, Bernie, and lived just up the road from us. She appeared at my back door one afternoon with a basket of clothes that she had taken off my line. Bernie had sent her to our house to get a tractor part from Lorne, but as she drove in the lane, dark storm clouds loomed overhead, looking like they were going to burst open any minute. Seeing my clothesbasket sitting under the line, Nancy rushed over, grabbed the basket and quickly retrieved the clothes from the line. I had been busy sewing that day and didn't notice the dark clouds outside. So when Nancy appeared at my back door with the basket of clothes and introduced herself, I just naturally invited her in.

We immediately hit it off and became instant friends, and have remained so ever since. Nancy was my lifeline in the early years of my marriage. As I couldn't drive, Nancy took me to many places that I never would have gotten to otherwise. We went shopping together, to auction sales, church events, funerals and, yes, even to a rock concert (which you will read about later in my book). We babysat for each other and visited often over the years.

Nancy had six children, three boys and three girls. They were close in age to my children, so we spent a lot of time visiting at each other's home. In the winter, while the kids watched TV and ate popcorn, we four adults played cards. In the summer, we'd have campfires, with wiener and marshmallow roasts for the kids. They loved it! We celebrated birthdays together (still do) and anniversaries, and many other family events. When my mother lived with us and I needed help with her, it was always Nancy who helped me out and was there for me.

We had a lot of laughs together over the years, such as the time we went to pick rhubarb at Lorne's old homestead across the road from Nancy's house. We had loaded the back seat of Nancy's Volkswagen Beetle with so much rhubarb – leaves and all – that we could hardly find our kids who were also in the back seat. Thank goodness we didn't have to go far and, luckily, there were no seat belts laws back then.

Another time, Nancy introduced me to my first auction sale. As I had never been to an auction before, I didn't know what to expect, and I also didn't have much money to spend. But when I saw the auctioneer holding up two lamps, I decided I wanted one of them for my livingroom, so I raised my hand. Soon the auctioneer hollered, "Sold! To the lady over there," pointing at me. Before long, someone brought over not one, but two, lamps. I paid him for the two lamps but was sick inside as I wondered how I was going to tell Lorne that I spent our hard-earned money on two lamps when we only needed one. As it turned out though, on the way home, one got broken, so I only had one to show him. And Lorne never did ask what I paid for it. Nancy and I had a lot of laughs over that one.

Over the years, we watched each other's children grow into adults and marry. Now, we're watching their children grow into adults and marry. And so, the life cycle continues.

The following story excerpt, I wrote as an English assignment while taking a course at Conestoga College, 1981.

> I have two very close friends. While others I have
> met over the years have drifted in and out of my life,
> these two people have remained my loyal and constant
> friends.

First, there is Nancy – short, chubby, happy-go-lucky. Nancy is always smiling and always happiest wearing a pair of old, faded blue jeans with a baggy, scruffy shirt. She is one who is always more concerned about the other person's welfare than she is about her own. She would gladly give the shirt off her back, if need be, to help another fellow in need.

Kind and thoughtful, Nancy is never one to forget my birthday, anniversary, or Christmas. She is always the first to phone on those special occasion days and say, "Happy birthday, Bev." Or whatever else the occasion calls for. Although a high school dropout, Nancy's common-sense approach to problems and life in general shows a remarkable intelligence.

Then there is Sandy, a more reserved individual who is always exquisitely dressed and beautifully coordinated. Although Sandy has a husband and family of three, she is never too busy to give me a call to see how I'm doing. Whenever she comes into town to shop, she always manages a quick visit for a chat before returning home. Sandy, too, would help out at a moment's notice if ever I needed help.

I feel fortunate to have two very dear friends that I know I can rely on and I hope they feel the same way about me.

29

❦

The Next Few Years

Many things happened over the next few years. Lorne's mom passed away January 7, 1966, in her 65th year. She lay down in the afternoon for a nap and never woke up. It was quite a shock to everyone. I phoned my mom to see if she could come and stay with the kids while Lorne and I went to the funeral home. But as I was ironing my clothes to wear to the funeral home, I was overcome with such severe stomach pains, I could barely walk. It felt like someone was ripping my stomach apart. Lorne quickly phoned Nancy and she rushed me to the doctor and, from there, to the hospital, as Lorne had to stay home with the kids.

I remember the nurses at the hospital discussing where to put me, on the first or second floor. Even though I was doubling up in pain, I told them I couldn't stay because my mother-in-law died and I had to go to the funeral. I thought they'd give me something for pain and send me home again. The hospital was the last place I wanted to be at that moment. But sometimes in life, we don't have much choice over things. That was one of those times.

The next few days were a blur. I had had a gallbladder attack and a very inflamed pancreas, was in an oxygen tent, and on heavy medication for 2-3 days before I finally started coming around. Lorne said the doctor told him I was in a very serious condition and had a nurse stay with me at all times, even through the night. The nurses took shifts sitting by my bed during the time I was in an oxygen tent. I always felt bad that I never made it to my mother-in-law's funeral. She truly was a super lady!

In the spring of 1972, I decided to get a job. In hindsight, I think I was kind of pressured into it. I was sick of people always asking me if I worked or not. With five kids and a large house and garden to look after, what else is there? Anyway, I applied at Campbell Soup in Listowel and was hired part time. I drove into work and back with Mary B. and her mother from Hesson because, as yet, I still didn't have a driver's license.

I only lasted two months there, long enough to buy myself a new sewing machine. Then I quit. I always had to rely on Mary to take me to work and back. At Campbell's, I was on a "call-in" basis. Whenever they needed someone, they would call the night before and want me to come in the next day. I hated that. I would have to quickly phone Mary to see if I could ride with her. Then I would have to rush around to get things done at home. I preferred a job where I knew exactly the days I had to work, so I could plan my week around them. Finally, I decided all the aggravation wasn't worth it. (I was also becoming a basket case.) The only thing nice about working at Campbell Soup was the pay cheque. I sure missed that.

On May 27, 1972, Lorne's father died in his 74th year. He died in the hospital from a respiratory illness. He had had asthma and breathing problems all his life.

The summer of 1972, I decided to try and get my driver's license. While my neighbour, Dorothy, watched Sharon and Bill for me, a driving instructor from town came out to the farm to give me lessons. The day of my third lesson, we had driven into town as usual when the instructor asked me to pull into the license bureau for a minute. I didn't think much of it at the time, thinking he had to pick something up at the office. When he got back in the car, he informed me that I was going to take my driving test – right away! I was flabbergasted. Only the day before, I had wondered aloud to Lorne that maybe I was wasting my time, that maybe I would never learn to drive. Well, I took my test, and passed, even though to this day I still cannot parallel park.

All those years we lived on the farm, I always had to rely on someone to take me when I wanted to go someplace. Now, I was free to drive myself. I was deliriously happy and walked on air for quite a few days. A whole new world, it seemed, was now opening up for me.

At first, I didn't drive very much because I was still plenty nervous on the road. Brian was in high school, Grade 12, by this time and played football after school. Because of his after-school practices, he always missed the bus home. I would have to pick him up after school. Driving to Listowel and back 3-4 times a week though, soon gave me the confidence to venture out more.

One day, with all the kids crammed in the car, I headed for Kitchener. I had never driven on the expressway before as I always took the back roads. This time, as I was heading toward Kitchener, I asked the kids, "Should I take the expressway or not?" They all hollered, "Go for it, Mom. Go for it!" From then on, I was unstoppable.

February 21, 1973, my father died. By this time, the kids were older and I was working three days a week as a can winder at Spinrite Yarns in Listowel, and loving it. But Dad's death left me so devastated that I quit there too, after only working a few months.

In 1976, I took a typing course one night a week at Conestoga College in Waterloo. In 1977, I enrolled again for a fulltime bookkeeping course. I received my certificate August 3, 1978.

Around 1979, Mom sold her house in Kitchener and moved in with us. We built an addition onto the back of the house, above the garage. Her apartment consisted of two very large rooms, divided into a livingroom on one side and a bedroom/dinette on the other. By this time, Mom was having a bit of difficulty walking, so it seemed like the perfect arrangement to have her move in with us. Around this time, I was also again working part time, now at the Listowel Banner, the newspaper office in town. I started out by collating newspapers, eventually working my way a few years later into the office. Lorne was now working at Uniroyal in Elmira.

30

❧

University

In 1983, I started taking courses at Waterloo University. To be admitted as a non-degree student, I had to first have an interview with the Dean. I did, and was accepted. I took "Introduction to Essay Writing" as my first course. I decided on this course because I'd always liked English in school. Also, I felt that if I was going to take university courses, I would be writing a lot of essays, so it seemed the perfect course for a starter.

Going to university was a whole new experience for me. Not only was I forty-six years old, I was old enough to be the other students' mother. Plus I only had a grade nine education. All the other students were high school graduates. Also, I was only a non-degree student, whereas the others were all working toward a degree.

For my first assignment, we had to read a certain poem, analyze it, and then give a summary of the poem in class the following week. When I read the poem, I couldn't understand any of it. Absolutely nothing at all in the poem made any sense to me. I was so upset about it, I was ready to quit then and there, thinking I must be really stupid. But because I had already paid big bucks to take the course – and because I feel that once you start something, you should always finish it – I decided to go back the following week and see what the other students had to stay about the poem.

The following week, the professor started on his lecture, as usual. Half way through, though, he casually asked the class how many had finished their assignment from the week before. Not a hand went up. No one could understand the poem. The professor then laughed, said he just threw that in to give everyone a scare.

Shortly after, we had to write a poem of our own for a homework assignment. The poem wasn't supposed to rhyme. This was my first poem...

THE TRANSFORMATION

Withered from arthritis and old age
She shuffles along, cane in hand.
The children see her coming and say,
"Here comes a witch!"
She reaches them, pauses, and smiles.
The children view her again, momentarily
And smile back.
Unknowingly, the old woman has created a transformation.

I ended the course with a C+ average. Not much, I know, but when compared my mark with the other marks posted, I was at the mid-point. Not bad, I thought, considering I only had a grade nine education. My marks were higher than many of the students who were graduates, so I felt pretty good.

My next course, though, was psychology, much harder. I found it to be very demanding – enormous amounts of reading and studying to do. By this time, Brian was also engaged to be married and his fiancé, Gidget L., had asked me to make her wedding gown. I decided then that taking university courses with my limited education, plus trying to sew a wedding gown, keeping up with my housework, and looking after Mom and my family, was just too much.

I did finish the course though, but decided that before taking any more university courses, I needed to upgrade my education and get my secondary diploma. So, shortly after that, I enrolled at the Independent Learning Centre in Toronto and started taking correspondence courses. For the first while, whenever I finished a course, I had to write an exam at the local high school. After I reached a certain age, however, I didn't have to go to the high school to write the test. They just sent it to me and, after writing it, I would send it back to the school for marking. There was no way that one could cheat on the test because it was worded in such a way that you had to have studied the material to know the answer. For instance, in one English course, I had to read a book and the questions were based on that book.

Fifteen (long) courses later, on April 2, 1993, I finally received my Secondary School Diploma. Many times along the way, I was tempted to give up, but now I'm glad I didn't. Getting that diploma in the mail was like winning the lottery. After ten long years of taking correspondence courses, it meant everything to me.

Shortly after I received my diploma, my daughter, Donna, sent me a cute, fuzzy, little teddy bear wearing a blue graduation cap with a yellow tassel. I was so overwhelmed when I received that bear, not because it was cute, although it was, but for what it represented – all my years of hard work. I cried that day. Donna was the only one who actually acknowledged my efforts with a gift of congratulations. That bear still sits on my bedroom dresser today and I treasure it as much as the day I received it.

31

Writing Aspirations

In 1986, I happened to see a small ad in *The Listowel Banner* advertising a freelance writing course being offered in the town of Drayton, about a half hour drive from home. It sounded interesting, so I signed up. I had always wanted to write and had had very good marks on all my writing assignments while taking correspondence courses. So I thought, "What the heck. I may as well give it a shot."

It turned out to be the best move I ever made. I loved it! There were only four of us taking the course, so we were a pretty tight group. Our instructor, Jean Neiderer, was superb in explaining the ins and outs of writing.

Every week, we had to write a story and bring it into class the following week to be read aloud for everyone to hear. Then we each had to give our opinion of what we thought of the story. Our instructor stressed at the beginning of the course that we be honest with each other and, I believe, we were.

On the last day of classes, our assignment was to write a short story about the course, within half an hour's time. This is what I had written:

FINAL

Tonight is the final night. Once a week for the past seven weeks, four of us have gathered together in the small community of Drayton for a freelance course. At the beginning, we were four complete strangers with one common bond: a desire to write. During these few weeks, we have become friends with each other, laughed with each other, and even divulged a bit of our lives with each other.

I know, for instance, that Valerie loves horses and she has a hunk of a husband who whips around town in a small, foreign car. Glynis has small, inquisitive children who seem to have a keen interest in camels. Andy is a helicopter enthusiast and also a teacher who hates homework. I bet his students think he's the greatest.

Jean is the instigator of this group. She diligently led us through the basics of freelancing. She told us the bad and the good of it. She even endured the countless questions I bombarded her with every week. Jean has inspired us all.

Each of us will leave here tonight with the hope of putting our new-found knowledge to work, of putting our byline in print.

Yes, this is the final night, but it may be a new beginning.

Thank you, Jean.

Although the course only lasted seven weeks, by the time it ended, the girls were calling me Erma Bombeck, after a very popular writer of a syndicated column. That gave me the encouragement I needed to try my hand at writing. I submitted my first story to the Listowel *Independent* newspaper a few weeks later. On Monday, August 18, 1986, I had my first story published. Although it was only for a small paper, I was as proud as a peacock that day. I actually saw my byline in print! As for the others in the class, Glynis went on to work for the Elmira paper, writing a humorous weekly column. Valerie, as of this writing, still continues to write for the *K-W Record*. And Andy, well, I lost touch with him.

32

First Published Story

Here's my first story in the Listowel *Independent*.

FREE – TO A GOOD HOME!
By Beverly J. Vollmer

The ad read, "Free – to a good home. Short-haired kittens."

"What do you think?" my husband questioned, glancing up from his morning paper. "Do you think we should get one? Those darn mice have been getting in the granary, eating the grain, destroying the feed bags. We definitely need a cat to clean up the mice around the barn."

"Okay by me," I replied. And that's how Cookie, our beautiful orange tabby cat came to live with us. I explained to the kids that Cookie could live temporarily in the garage until she became familiar with her surroundings. Then, she would have to be transferred to the barn.

Eagerly, the kids prepared a bed for her. Reluctantly, I prepared the litter box.

In the ensuing months, Cookie became the most pampered cat in the neighbourhood. Rich, warm milk, straight from the cow, and the best of table scraps became her diet. She was cuddled, brushed, petted and played with seven days a week. It was understandable, then, that Cookie's transition to the barn in the fall was not an easy one for her.

Her days as a pampered feline were now over, but Cookie wasn't destined to be a loner. By spring, I noticed she had a friend constantly with her, a large, gray Tom cat that looked in worse shape than the stuffed puppy my three year old carried around every day. The kids were happy that Cookie had found a friend; I wasn't.

Eventually, it became obvious that Cookie was going to be a mother. The kids were overjoyed with the news. Late that summer, Cookie had her first Litter – Muffy, Fluffy, Ginger, Tabby, and Stripey – so named by my two preschoolers.

"What are we going to do with all these cats?" I asked my husband one day.

"Dunno," he replied.

That winter, Fluffy, Muffy, Ginger and Tabby explored their new surroundings. Poor Stripey, though, never made it through the winter. He met a terrible fate on the highway one night.

Like rabbits, our cats rapidly multiplied. Late the next fall, Cookie, Fluffy, and Muffy each had a litter – fourteen kittens in all.

"What are we going to do with all these cats?" I asked my husband again, now with apprehension in my voice.

"Dunno," he replied. After that, litters of kittens appeared with increasing frequency around the barn. The kids were no longer enthused. They answered with a "so what" whenever I told them about any new litters.

Before long, the cats started making their way to the house. They were everywhere – on the porch, on the window sills, in the flower beds, on the hood of the car, and climbing up the screen doors. I even stumbled over them while hanging out the wash. The cats were driving me crazy!

"What are we going to do with all these cats?" I screamed at my husband.

"Dunno," he replied. "Maybe...maybe we could sneak up on some of our enemies some dark night and drop off a few. Or maybe we could...I've got it!" He snapped his fingers. Grabbing a pen and a note pad off the kitchen table he began writing, "Free – to a good home. Short-haired kittens..."

33

Further Publications

After that first story appeared, I had countless people around Listowel telling me how much they enjoyed my story, so I wrote another one, and another. Following are some of my endeavours at writing.

This story appeared in the Listowel *Independent* on September 8, 1986.

WHAT A QUESTION TO ASK
By Beverly J. Vollmer

Normally, I am a calm, very relaxed person. Even under pressure, with a little effort, I usually managed to keep my cool. But there are three words in the English language that, when combined as a question, set my adrenalin roaring, my blood pressure soaring, and my whole body gyrating like an overloaded washer in the spin cycle. I have come to detest this question even more than the buttered turnips I was forced to eat as a kid. The button that triggers this emotional upheaval in me are the words, "Do you work?"

"Do you work?" I reiterate mentally: Of course not! I bide my time doodling in the telephone directly while talking on the phone to other bored housewives like me who also don't work. I lock myself in my dimly lit closet and play tiddlywinks with my shadow. I lie on the couch all day and fantasize about Tom Selleck.

"Do you work?" Those words are the ultimate in bad manners. Doesn't every housewife who has a husband, an elderly mother living with her, five robust grandchildren who visit regularly, who takes correspondence courses and has a seven-room, two-storey house with an attached garage work?

"Do you work?" Twice in the past month I've been asked that revolting question. Both times, I've managed to control the vibrating deep within me and sweetly answer, "No, I don't work." But I can't continue under false pretenses much longer. A time will come when some clod will ask, "Do you work?" and I know the combustion in me will cause an internal explosion. Then, instead of meekly answering, "No, I don't work," I will instead gaze directly into my interrogator's eyes and madly scream, "Of course I work. I do, I do, I do!"

This story appeared in the Listowel *Independent*, September, 1986 (exact date unknown).

PUT THE JOY BACK IN YOUR LIFE
By Beverly J. Vollmer

To some people, joy is winning a lottery. To others, it's a slow parachute descent to earth from 2500 feet above ground. To still others, it's the simple pleasures of life – gazing at a rainbow or watching a sunset. To me, joy is going out for supper.

I hate cooking. Don't get me wrong; I'm not a terrible cook. I can whip up such fancy delights as trout in champagne sauce or coq au vin just as easy as the best of chefs. At times, the smells coming from my oven are just as appealing as those coming from Betty Crocker's.

But after cooking three meals a day, 365 days a year for 32 years, minus the days spent in hospital during childbirth, attending wedding receptions and sick days when I was too weak to cook, I figure it all adds up to approximately 34,000 meals I've cooked in my lifetime. Not added to this figure are the thousands of snacks I've prepared for my husband while he was glued to the tube watching *Hockey Night in Canada* and all the bedtime snacks I prepared for my kids.

Is it any wonder I hate to cook? Many times I cooked meals for large threshing gangs who had insatiable appetites after working long hours in the hot sun. Large family gatherings, which require enormous amounts of food to be prepared, are also a constant occurrence at my house. Many times I spent helping out at church to prepare for some special church dinner, only to come home and cook again for my own brood.

Another reason I hate cooking is because it is a barrier

between me and the svelte 34-24-34 figure I would like to be. Who can resist the temptation to nibble when the aroma of Hungarian cabbage rolls cooking in mother's old-fashioned tomato sauce drifts across the kitchen? Who can resist cutting the crust off a freshly baked loaf of bread and smothering it in butter, just for taste?

I haven't always hated cooking. As a young bride, I took great delight in preparing new dishes. I spent long hours paging through magazines and cookbooks looking for exotic recipes to prepare. Many young brides are very apprehensive about cooking for the first time. My theory was that if you can read a recipe, you can cook.

Somewhere along the way though, my enthusiasm waned. I have never been able to recapture that old feeling. I have tried, but failed. I even bought a microwave with the hope that if I changed my way of cooking, my enthusiasm would return. It didn't.

Tonight my husband is taking me out for supper. He's such a sweet, understanding guy. He knows how to put the joy back into my life.

This story appeared in the Listowel *Independent* September 13, 1986.

FROM PUSSYCAT TO BEAST
By Beverly J. Vollmer

In a few weeks, wives everywhere will lose their husbands when they succumb to the forceful grip of *Hockey Night in Canada*. Under its hold, husbands undergo a drastic transformation. Hockey has been known to change any man from the gentlest of pussycats into a ferocious wild beast.

Ladies, don't try to rescue your husbands. They don't want to be saved. They'll come back when *Hockey Night in Canada*, like a mighty eagle, releases its talons and the Stanley Cup is returned to the shelf.

Mind you, your husband will still share the same house with you, will still be underfoot, as usual, and will still have the same physical appearances. But when the game is on – BEWARE! He becomes oblivious to his surroundings and his whole being focuses on the boob tube, like an animal ogling his prey.

At this time, it is wise to avoid your husband, as any distractions will immediately bring out the beast in him. Take up a hobby or go on a trip; come back in the spring. He won't even know you're gone, as long as you stock up the fridge before you leave.

If getting away isn't feasible, your only alternative is to try and observe the following ten rules. They won't change the beast any, but they might increase your chances of survival.

Ten Rules for Wives While Hockey is in Progress

1. Never walk in front of the TV, not even on tippy toes. To do so would really bring out the beast in your husband.
2. Save the juicy bit of news about the car's dented fender until morning when the game is over.
3. Never rattle dishes or use the vacuum cleaner. The latter is definitely a no-no – it absolutely drives ALL men wild!
4. Put the kids to bed as soon as the game begins.
5. Only buy beer with twist-off caps – openers get lost.
6. Never speak to your husband when the puck is anywhere near the goal post.
7. Never interrupt (or argue) with him when he wildly proclaims, "Why that dirty rotten...!"
8. Keep the dog quiet. Put a muzzle on him. (On the dog, I mean, although your husband could probably benefit from one too.)
9. Never – under any circumstances – call him to the phone during hockey play. If his team scores while he's away, he'll remind you about it forever.
10. And last, but not least, don't try to divert his attention away from the screen by wearing a sexy negligee. He won't even notice.

This story appeared in the Listowel *Independent*, September 29, 1986.

LIFE BEGINS AT 40
By Beverly J. Vollmer

Many articles have been written over the years on how life begins at forty. Writers would have you believe that forty is a marvelous age – lots of free time, bus excursions every year, no worries or cares. The list goes on and on. They make it sound as though the first thirty-nine years of one's life are spent in a cocoon. Then, at forty, you emerge like a Monarch butterfly into the big, wide, wonderful world.

Well, I hate to explode a myth, but it just isn't so. The only resemblance between a life beginning at forty and a real birth is the fact that you cry – because suddenly a look in the mirror reveals gray hairs, crow's feet, wrinkles, and a crêpey neck. Yuk!

It is also the age when pot bellies, double chins, droopy bust lines become part of the scenario. Your waistline merges with your hips, and joints creak in time with the music of Jane Fonda. At forty, skin loses its firmness. When your husband gives you a love pat on your tush, it still jiggles thirty seconds later.

At forty, there are grandchildren – bless their little warm hearts. They frazzle your nerves more at this age than at any other. When your own kids were small, you could deal with tantrums, hair pulling, screaming, biting, name calling. But now...

At forty, energy dwindles. In your youth, you could party all night without any side effects. A mile or two of jogging was no sweat. But now, at forty, just a trot to the corner store feels like a marathon run.

Free time? Forget it! There isn't any. You're either

cleaning, cooking or shopping (all of which takes twice as long now) or trying to cope with Gramma or Gramps who, by this time, have probably moved in with you.

Second career? The only second career you'll have is that of babysitter. Your kids will bring their little darlings home for a short visit and then forget to pick them up again.

Sounds all negative? Well, life at forty does have one positive aspect – no more zits.

*

When this article first appeared, one woman wrote into *Points of View* and lambasted me for such a negative article. I was dumbfounded because I really didn't think anyone would take the article seriously. Apparently though, someone did.

Remember earlier , I mentioned my friend, Nancy? Well, in 1986 I took her to a rock concert at Centre in the Square in Kitchener. I wrote this article for the Listowel *Independent*, but the date it was published is unknown.

HER EARSPLITTING INTRO INTO ROCK
By Beverly J. Vollmer

Most teenagers would be delighted to receive a free ticket to a rock concert, but when it's offered to a woman over 40, well, the enthusiasm isn't quite the same. Ask my friend, Nancy. She knows.

I phoned her the other day to offer her the free ticket if she'd accompany me to the rock concert in which my son, Brian, was the lead singer. My husband had previously planned on going but, unfortunately, he had a severe bout of flu and cancelled out at the last minute. The only person I could think of who was around my age and who "just might" go to a rock concert with me was Nancy.

"A rock concert?" Nancy questioned suspiciously.

"That's right," I replied. "Brian gave us two tickets for tonight's performance, but Lorne can't make it. Will you go with me?"

Silence..."Bev, are you serious?" Nancy questioned again.

"Sure, why not?"

More silence..."Well, I was going to play volleyball at the gym tonight, but..."

"The free ticket includes a back stage pass," I quickly interrupted, trying to arouse excitement.

"Well, alright. Boy, wait 'til Tim hears about this!" (Tim is Nancy's 16-year-old son.) An hour later, the two of us were on our way to the rock concert.

As soon as Nancy and I emerged from our car, the stares began. We felt as though we were aliens from another planet. It wasn't just our age that stood out among the teenagers, our clothes, too, were conspicuous; no match for body-hugging blue jeans and tight leathers of the teen crowd. One girl snickered at us, then turned to her pals and said, "Do you suppose they got their nights mixed up?" Her friends giggled in unison.

Once inside the entertainment centre, I bought Nancy a gin and tonic. I thought a tranquilizer was just what she needed to prepare for the ear-popping music to follow. I was familiar with the sound level of rock music because my husband and I frequently attended the band's gigs when they played in the area, but Nancy, I knew, was not. She had never been to a rock concert before. She was soon to learn what they were all about.

Soon after we settled into our balcony seats, the lights dimmed and the music began. Very slowly...very softly...at first, BUT THEN...all hell broke loose! The sound of the drums and guitars and my son's deep alto voice blasted from the speakers with more force than Hurricane Hazel.

People clapped and swayed to the beat of the music, completely oblivious of its heightening volume. The louder the sounds, the more frenzied the audience became. Lighters flickered everywhere, a gesture of approval to the band. The atmosphere was electrifying.

I looked at Nancy, her mouth ajar, her eyes bulging, a look of shock written over her face. She turned to speak, but changed her mind, realizing it was hopeless.

When the concert ended, I didn't bother to mention the back stage passes to Nancy. She wouldn't have heard me anyway. She was too busy poking her fingers into her ears, trying to clear out the ringing.

This story appeared in the Listowel *Independent*, October 13, 1986.

THE CRAZY BABIES
By Beverly J. Vollmer

A few years ago, five local women formed a rock group known as The Crazy Babies. They became an overnight success.

I remember their first performance...the tension...the jitters...the excitement...the scurrying around back stage during last-minute preparations. Someone peeked between the curtains for a glimpse of the audience; the hall was filled to capacity.

Soon, the concert was ready to begin; a hush fell on the crowd. Then, five Crazy Babies came rockin' 'n rolling onto the stage, like five Mexican jumping beans just released from a paper sack.

Kitty, the leader of the group, welcomed the crowd and quickly brought them to a partying mood with her quick wit and bubbly personality. She introduced the band. Besides herself on guitar, there was Tootsie on drums, Babes on the "pops," and Susie and Betsy, the go-go girls.

The Crazy Babies definitely weren't your typical rock 'n roll band. Clad in a mixture of garb from the '50s and '80s, they appeared...different!

Tootsie wore a pair of oversized sunglasses, a long-sleeved white shirt, black vest, and rolled-up blue jeans, revealing a pair of knee-high socks with the toes boldly identifiable in bright, flashy colours. (No shoes!) Perched on top of her head was an enormous red bow.

Babes also wore sunglasses, plus an old Paddyfest hat that looked like it had been salvaged from the dump.

From holes in its sides, extended two, thick, long golden braids entwined with red ribbons.

Kitty wore a flared skirt and a '50s T-shirt with matching knee socks. A large turquoise bonnet adorned her head. She looked every bit "a crazy baby."

The go-go girls, Susie and Betsy, resembled two Barbie dolls ready for a Halloween party in their mini-skirts, tights, dark glasses and bows. Each member of the group also wore a Crazy Baby apron.

The Crazy Babies gave an excellent performance with their zany antics and rock 'n rollin' to the beat of music from the '50s: "Rock Around The Clock," "Peppermint Twist," and "Clap Your Hands." They did act a bit crazy, but after all, they had their name to live up to.

The crowd was ecstatic. Although no one flicked their Bic or stood on chairs yelling, "Encore!" the Crazy Babies knew the crowd loved them. It was evident by all the happy faces. If Tina Turner had been there, she surely would have asked for their autograph.

The last set had to be cut short. An unexpected telegram arrived from The Sugar Daddies asking The Crazy Babies to accompany them the next day to Las Vegas for an engagement.

As a last adieu, The Crazy Babies discarded their aprons to an excited crowd who were eager for a memento of the occasion.

After the crowd dispersed, the local paper came and took pictures. Then, five tired but happy Crazy Babies went home. Their first...and only...performance was over.

Soon the lights went out...the church doors closed...the fall church social was over.

I remember the night well...for I was one of those Crazy Babies.

Sometime around 1987-88, Lorne and I took a trip to New York City with George and Rita, Lorne's sister and her husband. When we returned, I sent the following story to *The Listowel Banner*.

A VIEW OF NEW YORK CITY
By Beverly J. Vollmer

Home Sweet Home – an old adage maybe, but one that holds significant meaning for me since returning recently from a four-day bus trip to New York City, along with my husband, sister-in-law and brother-in-law. New York City – an unforgettable experience – but one that left me more appreciative of all the things I generally take for granted.

We arrived in the Big Apple, as it is commonly called, around 8:30 on a Friday evening, amidst row upon row of skyscrapers that towered endlessly into the clouds. Noise and commotion were evident everywhere.

New Yorkers and tourists flooded the sidewalks, and vendors stood on every street corner selling their wares, while massive traffic jams caused angry motorists to blast their horns. Sirens wailed. Strings of neon lights flashed brightly along the strips, beckoning people into the bars and discotheques.

Winos lay on the sidewalks while shopkeepers covered their windows for the night with bars and chains to keep out looters. In front of the shops, many of which were plastered with graffiti, were piles of garbage, the bags ripped open and the contents spewing into the street, giving off at times a nauseous odor.

We saw very little grass or shrubbery in New York City, except occasionally on balconies or in the very small parks that are sandwiched between the skyscrapers. Central Park is an exception, with its 850 acres of greenery. No houses could be seen either, just an abundance of high rises and skyscrapers.

Our driver, Paul, had instructed us briefly on what never to do while in New York City. Never go out alone, stay in groups; never go anywhere unless it's in a yellow New York City cab. "If it isn't yellow or doesn't have New York City written on it, don't get in," he warned.

In New York City, you hail a cab by raising your arm. And don't worry about not finding one. They're everywhere. They cruise the streets 24 hours a day; usually you'll find them zooming in and out of traffic like there is no tomorrow. You don't have to wonder about fares, prices are boldly written on the door: $1.50 initial charge, 25 cents per 1/5 mile, and 20 cents per minute for waiting and stopping.

If you drive your own car in New York City and stop at an intersection, don't be surprised if a boy darts out and washes your windows – whether you want them washed or not – and be prepared to pay him! No jaywalking either, unless you don't value your life.

NEVER SLEEPS

As we neared the entrance of our hotel room, my husband pointed out a cockroach that had scooted across our path from underneath a pile of garbage strewn along the sidewalk. And, not far away, I noticed a couple of winos curled up against the buildings, passersby oblivious to their existence.

Winos, derelict bums – whatever you want to call them – are common in New York City. You'll find them lying on the sidewalks or on benches or, as my sister-in-law saw one on a Sunday morning, lying across the steps of a large cathedral, while parishioners casually walked around him into church.

On another occasion, I saw one lying in a fetal position on the sidewalk near our hotel. He was vigorously scratching his head. As I moved in closer to snap his picture, the thickness of dirt and grime in his hair became obvious.

Our hotel lobby was fabulously decorated with broadloom rug and huge chandeliers, but our room, one of 1700 in the hotel and situated on the 14th floor, was shabbily decorated and stank from stale air. Sheer curtains on the window, supposedly white at one time, were filthy, and the board across the top of the window was faded and water-stained. A desk, bed, nightstand and a worn-out upholstered chair completed the décor.

As we tried to sleep, the noise of New York City rumbled throughout the night. Sirens continued to wail and, at one point, my husband and I distinctly heard a gun being fired – not just once, but three times.

Paul, our driver, had mentioned earlier that New York City is also known as "the city that never sleeps." He was right about that. And neither did we! Toward morning, the noise subsided a bit, but never died entirely.

SIGHTS

The second day of our visit, we saw some fantastic sights and landmarks, via the Circle Line, a sightseeing yacht which took us on a cruise around Manhattan Island, the Statue of Liberty (the world's tallest sculpture), Empire State Building, United Nations headquarters, Gracie Mansion (the official resident of New York City mayors), Yankee Stadium (home of the New York Yankees), Grant's Tomb, and many of New York City's famous bridges, such as the George Washington Bridge, the Brooklyn Bridge and the Manhattan Bridge.

We toured China Town, Times Square, The Bronx, Greenwich Village, Wall Street, The Bowery, Lower Manhattan and Strawberry Field in Central Park which was dedicated to John Lennon. Lennon's wife, Yoko Ono, had an apartment overlooking that area.

We also toured the elite district where famous celebrities, such as Jacqueline Kennedy Onassis, Mary Tyler Moore, Katherine Hepburn and Tiny Tim have apartments. Apartments in that particular area are bought, not rented, and prices range from $1M - $3M. And that doesn't include maintenance.

There is so much to see in New York City. It is definitely a place to visit. But to live there – no thanks! When we crossed the Peace Bridge into Canada on our journey home, I exhaled a great sign of relief. And, upon reaching Listowel once again, and seeing houses, trees, shrubbery and clean surroundings, I realized how truly fortunate I am to be living here.

34

A Few More Stories

I've added a few more stories here which I wrote for English correspondence courses, and thought you may enjoy reading them.

MY FANTASY

I dreamed there was a very large cloud floating lazily above me. In that cloud were all the things I wanted from life: my hopes, my goals, my aspirations. I struggled to reach it. It was so close, and yet, so out of my grasp. In desperation, I looked around for something to retrieve it. I saw a lasso. Aiming for the cloud, I twirled the lasso through the air. My plan had worked; the lasso entwined itself around the cloud. I pulled it gently backward. Just as I was about to reach up and grab its contents, the cloud burst open and a million tiny raindrops spewed forth. All my hopes and dreams were now being washed away in one fleeting moment. I cried.

All of a sudden, I awoke to find my forehead and pillow wet. Looking up, I saw the rain dripping down through a crack in the ceiling. My dream, I realized, was just a fantasy.

How nice if life could really be as simple as my dream, I thought. If we could just reach up and pluck from the sky all the things we want in our lives, like happiness, wealth, and success.

But reality isn't like that. We must work hard to achieve what's most important in our lives. We must set goals and continually strive to reach them, day by day. Only then will we succeed.

THE DAY I ALMOST DIED

Have you ever thought about dying? Have you ever been close to death? Well, I have, and let me tell you, it's totally unlike what you read about in the papers. Peaceful? Serene? Don't believe it – it's pure hell!

My trauma began innocently enough last year when I signed up for an "Effective Speaking" course. Had the brochure read "Public Speaking," I would have dismissed the idea immediately because the thought of speaking in public absolutely terrifies me.

But, *effective speaking*, well, that was different. I thought it would be a course covering proper grammar usage, choosing the right words, proper posture when talking, keeping eye contact, things of that nature. But that was not the case.

The first evening of the class, the instructor gave an outline of the course. When he came to the part, "I want everyone here tonight to take a turn to come to the front of the class and speak for three minutes about him or herself," a panic button went off in my brain.

Instantly, beads of perspiration trickled down my

forehead and my heart pounded like it had been struck by a million tom-toms. I silently wished that the instructor would start on the other side of the room. He did, but it didn't help any. In fact, it made matters worse. By the time he arrived at my side of the room, I was too weak to move. I felt my body slowly sliding down my chair, like a glob of Jell-O on a warm day.

At that moment, my mind seemed to be focusing on something – something I remembered reading once – about a woman who came back from the dead. She told of going through a long, black tunnel. At its end, she saw a magnificent light and someone was there calling her name, beckoning her.

I listened. I could hear someone too, only it was *my* name I heard. "Beverly, it's your turn now." I could hear the voice calling. That was the last thing I remembered before slipping into unconsciousness.

I'm back in the real world now. I guess I'll never really know for sure how close to dying I came that night. One thing I do know for sure though – no more Effective Speaking courses for me!

35

❦

Many Changes

By 1988, a lot of changes had already taken place. All our children were married now, and we already had seven grandchildren.

Donna was the first to get married. She married Michael (Angie) Costa on July 2, 1977. They had met on a blind date, arranged by her best friend, Shelley D., and hit if off right from the start. I remember the first time I met Angie, my first thought was, "Boy, he's really short!" After their honeymoon, they moved to Thunder Bay, Ontario, where Angie opened an auto body shop with his brothers.

I can still remember the day they left for Thunder Bay. They had come to the house in a truck owned by Angie's brother to pick up the remaining stuff of Donna's. With the truck loaded to the hilt with all their belongings and Donna waving goodbye to me out the side window, I suddenly felt a strange lump in my throat and a terrible heaviness in my heart as they drove slowly out the lane. I felt like I was never going to see her again.

Before long though, Lorne and I were looking forward to our trips to Thunder Bay. The first time we flew there, I remember looking out the plane's window after we landed and seeing Donna for the first time since their marriage, standing on the air strip, and my first thought then was, "Gosh, I didn't realize Donna was that short!"

Next to get married was Brian; he married Gidget L. on August 5, 1978. Mike was next, marrying Sylvia F., October 12, 1979, followed by Bill and Debra L. August 20, 1983. Charin was the last of our children to get married, on June 30, 1984, to Bernie. Unfortunately though, not all couples are compatible with each other, as was the case with Brian and Gidget. They eventually divorced and Brian later married Lynda C., August 10, 1991. Brian had one daughter, Jasmin, with his first wife. Charin and Bernie also divorced; they had no children; and Charin later married Greg R. on March 1, 1986.

In the fall of 1988, Mom's health deteriorated so much that I eventually had to put her in Knollcrest Lodge, a nursing home. She could no longer look after herself, could only walk with the aid of a walker, and was incontinent. And the house smelled so bad at times that I was embarrassed to invite anyone over. I was at a point where I could no longer cope with it all. Looking back now, I'm sure I would have had a nervous breakdown if I hadn't put her in Knollcrest when I did, but at the time I was very reluctant to put her there. It was only because of pressure from a VON nurse and my husband telling me that it was the best thing to do that I finally consented, but I had many guilt trips later on over my decision.

Earlier that year, I had phoned the VON for assistance in giving Mom a bath, as that was one thing I could not do. Mom was always very modest about her body and I was absolutely sure that she would never want me seeing her nude, let alone bathing her. Well, the VON nurse, Sharon J., came a few times and bathed Mom, then one day informed me that she could no longer come anymore. She said it wasn't safe for her, or me, to give Mom a bath, as one person could not lift her.

In the fall of 1988, Mom was admitted to Knollcrest. I remember that day well. When we left home, it was pouring cats and dogs. Mom was very quiet all the way to Knollcrest, and I felt so bad knowing she didn't want to go there that I could barely speak either. To make conversation, I tried to make it sound like it was a good thing, saying things like, "You'll be a lot happier there with people your own age," or

"It'll be better than sitting all day in your room by yourself," or "You'll have entertainment there," etc.

After she was admitted, I stayed for a while and then left, with the promise that I'd be back tomorrow to see her. The rain that I had encountered on the way there had changed to a blinding snowstorm by the time I left. Between the snow and my tears, I could barely see to drive home.

That fall, Lorne and I listed the farm with a real estate agent. Lorne was working now as a supervisor at Sundor, a canning factory in St. Jacobs, but he was finding it difficult trying to work the farm and working at the factory, too, so we made the decision to sell.

I was still taking correspondence courses at this time, and the following story is one I wrote for an English assignment, although it was never published.

MOVING ON

I watched, misty-eyed, as the real estate agent plunked the "For Sale" sign into the ground on our front lawn. Feelings of sadness overwhelmed me, and I felt a tremendous tightness in my chest as though my heart was breaking into a million pieces. "This is it," I thought, fighting back the tears, "There's no turning back now."

For the last few years, my husband and I had contemplated selling the old farmstead and moving into town. As we grew older and slower with each passing year, the work load around the farm had also seemed to increase. "What the heck do we want with such a big house anyway?" we questioned ourselves. Our children were married and gone now, and my husband held a good supervisor's position in a small canning factory nearby, so money was no problem either. And yet, as much as we both wanted to sell and move on, our roots had been firmly established in this community for thirty years, and making the decision to leave now was extremely difficult.

But then the drought came and our crops and grass-land smothered under the constant rays of the hot summer sun. My husband and I became tired and dis-couraged. We decided to sell. Although the drought wasn't the reason for our selling – we had been blessed with 29 very good years – it did give us the nudge we needed to take that first step, calling the real-estate agent.

Tears trickled down my cheeks now as I surveyed the yard around me – the well-cut lawn, the row of maples along the east fence, two ash trees centered di-rectly in front of the house, and the many flowers that adorned it all.

It hadn't always looked that way, I thought, my mind recalling how it had looked 30 years before when my husband and I, with three young children in tow, including a baby, moved in. The only landscaping back then consisted of weeds, a couple of Hawthorne trees, and one lilac bush. And the house itself was a complete shamble – unpainted and dilapidated, with a worn-out roof and many missing bricks. An old lean-to on the back of the house always reminded me of an old haunted house when the lights at night shone through its rickety-old barn boards.

But over the years, my husband and I had trans-formed the farm into a thing of beauty with our per-sistence and hard work. While my husband had planted grass and shrubs, tore out walls and windows and built cupboards and repaired the roof, I had papered and painted and dug up flower beds.

As I continued to gaze around the farm now, thirty years of memories seemed to unroll in front of me. The addition on the back of the house, it had been added ten years ago for Mom to live in after Dad had died. And the ash trees out front, Mom had brought them up from Kitchener when she moved in because she had wanted something to remind her of her home.

And the huge rock which sat in the front corner of the yard – I remembered how my husband had reluctantly placed it there with the front-end loader years ago, after I pleaded with him to bring it up from the back field. "It'll add beauty to the flower bed," I had told him.

And other things not quite so obvious stirred many memories in me. Like the mud puddles on the lane that my kids, as toddlers, loved to play in; and the west field where many a hockey game took place during the long winter months after our boys had made it into a skating rink. And the delight on the older children's faces as I arrived home from the hospital with baby number four. And again with baby number five. And the pathway leading from our house to the neighbours – the one that was so badly worn, I swore that nothing could possibly ever grow there again. And the time I looked out my kitchen window after just coming home from church and seeing my eight-year-old daughter whizzing by in her brother's go-cart and a cloud of dust, still wearing her white, first communion dress that only a few moments before she had worn to church.

And all the Christmases and Easters spent together as a family in this old house – and the weddings – what beautiful memories they all were! Of course there were bad times too, but they've been lost in the back of my memory as the happier ones unfold.

In a few weeks, strangers will go through our house and inspect the place, looking in cupboards and closets, peering into each room and surveying the area around them. But no matter how thoroughly they look, they will never see beyond the four walls – it takes thirty years of living here to do that!

36

Sold!

The following year – May, 1989 – the farm was sold. I was elated. I started a journal that very day and here are some excerpts from that journal. Note: Words in square brackets were not from the journal, but added later.

March 20, 1989 – Today [first day of spring] *we sold our farm to Mary and Gary Kocher. Very excited! Now I can make plans for our new house. Hurray!*

April 3, 1989 – Got a call from Shelley, my niece, this morning. Her mom, Leonne [my sister-in-law], passed away last night. The irony is that her birthday was on March 30.

April 4, 1989 – Got a phone call tonight while at the funeral home. Bill phoned to tell us that Deb had her baby, Kevin William, born at 5 this afternoon and weighing 7 lbs 15½ ounces. It's a funny feeling visiting someone that's just left the world and receiving a call about someone who's just entered.

April 10, 1989 – Tonight Sandy, my neighbour, and I went bowling. We came home in a blizzard. Could hardly see the road. Sandy nearly drove in the ditch. It was the first real storm we've had this month.

April 22, 1989 – Took a course in Doon today at Conestoga College on "How to Sell What You Write." I was terrified I'd never find the place. When I did find it, I still didn't know where to go, the college had so many buildings. I didn't know which one to enter. I thought I'd be late, but it turned out I was the first one there. Everyone was having just as hard a time to find the place as I did.

At night, Lorne and I went to St. Jacobs. Saw the play Waiting for the Parade. Excellent play, excellent cast!

April 23, 1989 – Had Bill, Deb, Ally and Kevin for supper. Mom was here too. She saw Kevin, the baby, for the first time. Nancy came over, then Rita and George. Still later, Albert R. and his boy came. After Rita and George left, Nancy helped me take Mom back to Knollcrest. Came home and started cleaning. Mary and Gary are coming tomorrow to look the place over again. I guess they want to check to make sure it looks the same when they move in. [They never did move in. They resold the farm to a Mennonite.]

April 24, 1989 – Mary and Bob Kocher came to look over the house one more time before signing the final papers. I doubt that they'll back out now – Mary seemed quite enthused.

Tonight was the last night of bowling for yet another year. Finished last, or close to it! Oh well, it was fun. Next Monday is our banquet.

April 26, 1989 – Went shopping to Fairview Mall and then to Conestoga Mall. Bought a pair of shoes and a few greeting cards. That was it. Brian phoned tonight and asked us to come for supper Sunday, said he would make it. Brian cook? I have to see it to believe it! I asked Lorne and he said we'd go.

Lucille Ball died today at age 77. Great actress and comedian.

April 30, 1989 – We had supper at Brian's today. He cooked. Was sure surprised. He had a very good meal. Saw Jasmine, Brian's daughter, too. I told *her she'd better come for a holiday this summer as it will be the last one on the farm. She seemed sad that we were leaving the farm.*

May 1, 1989 – Money came through on the house today. NOW we can start our plans for the house. Can hardly wait, although Lorne doesn't seem to be in any hurry. I wished he shared my enthusiasm.

Tonight was our bowling banquet. It's all over for another year. I didn't get any trophies, just a crying towel, pen and a deck of cards.

May 21, 1989 – Lorne and I went to see Aunt Priscilla today at Conestoga Lodge. Was surprised to see her looking so well for 90 years of age. She was also very alert. I got Lorne to take my picture with her. Can hardly wait to see how it turns out. We also went to see Sheldon, Lorne's brother. Had supper at Harvey's. Later in the evening, I went to see Mom at Knollcrest. Lorne stayed home and cut the lawn.

May 25, 1989 – Today was hell! We were involved in a car crash. Front end of our Chevette was smucked! Mom and I went to Stratford Hospital by ambulance. My knee cap was ripped open and had to have eight stitches to close the wound. Also have intense pain in my neck and chest. Poor Mom had a broken hip and had to have emergency surgery tonight. Lorne and I stayed at hospital until the operation was over. Nurses were amazed at how well she came through the operation.

Lorne had a lump and scrape on forehead, but otherwise alright. I'm thankful that no one was killed. This is the second head-on crash I've been in. Will never forget the sound of metal crushing.

[Lorne and I had been on our way to London with Mom to see a specialist about her walking problem. We got as far as Stratford when we stopped at a red light on Lorne Avenue. We were in the outside lane and a large van was beside us in the centre lane, with his front end sticking out past our little Chevette. Coming in the other direction was a pickup truck, whose driver was planning on making a left-hand turn. Because of the large van beside us, the driver of the pickup truck did not see our Chevette and, when the light turned green, the van beside us took off and immediately the pickup truck driver proceeded to make his turn and crashed into us, the impact sending Mom, who was in the back, crashing into the front seat and me into the dash.

Mom and I were taken by ambulance to Stratford Hospital, while a woman police office drove Lorne (who was carrying two women's purses – mine and Mom's) to the hospital. Lorne later had to get one of the kids to come and take us home as our car was a complete write-off.]

May 26, 1989 – Went to see Mom today. I'm amazed at how well she's improved. She asked for ice cream. Can hardly believe it!

May 27, 1989 – Went to see Mom again. Today she looked terrible. She was having a blood transfusion. Her mind was out of it today. She talked about shopping at Towers, etc. The nurses, though, said this was normal considering all the medication she'd had.

May 28, 1989 – Mom looked a bit better today. She was actually sitting up in bed. Edna and Fred were visiting her. Mike and Sylvia came in later with Adam and Michelle.

May 29, 1989 – I didn't go to the hospital today. I phoned instead. The nurse said Mom was weak, but otherwise okay. They tried to get her to walk today, but the nurse said they were unsuccessful in this, her first attempt.

I cleaned Mom's rooms today. Also, emptied her one dresser. It was very sad to go through the mementos she'd saved over the years. I hated to do it, but knew it had to be done. Life is cruel at times.

[After the car accident, Mom could no longer walk at all, and Knollcrest Lodge refused to take her back, stating that she needed too much nursing care. The hospital then sent her to Caressant Care in Harriston (against my wishes) because Caressant Care in Listowel was full. She spent about 16 months there before getting into Caressant Care in Listowel.]

August 7, 1989 – Today Donna had her baby, a boy, Vincent Michael, at 4 p.m. A day late for Charin's birthday. Everyone at the Costa residence is very excited. Donna comes home tomorrow and is having a cleaning service come in for the week.

September 29, 1989 – Went back to work today! First time in ten years. Felt wonderful. Working on a computer.

I also went to my first Junior B game tonight. The score at the end of the first period was 6-6. They went into overtime and Listowel scored in the last eleven seconds to win the game. I'm on the Listowel Hockey Women's Auxiliary so the photographer was there during the game to take our picture.

37

The Jr. B Cat

Every farm usually has lots of cats, and ours was no exception. Being the animal lover that I am, the first thing I thought about after knowing our farm was sold was what to do with all the cats. If the new owners didn't move in right away, I knew the older cats would probably venture over to the farm next door, which was okay by me; but it was the two Persian kittens in the barn and the one non-quite-so-grown-up cat that I worried about. I told hubby that we have to start looking for homes for them.

After telling my neighbour, Sandy, about the two Persian kittens in the barn that I wanted to home, she suggested the new people who moved in across the road from her might want some kittens. She said they already had a cat for a house pet, but they loved cats and just might want more for the barn. Well, after seeing the two fluffy Persian kittens, they immediately wanted them – but not for the barn. They wanted them as house pets, too. I sure was happy about that. Now there was only the one not-quite-so-grown-up cat to worry about.

Then the idea hit...The Jr. B hockey team was having an auction sale at the arena soon. Why not take the cat along and see if I could auction him off there?

So, the day of the sale, on a Saturday morning when hubby was busy in the barn (I didn't dare tell him my plans!) I sneaked the cat into the house, brushed him until his fur glistened, then tied a big red bow around his neck. Now, this cat had never been in the house before, and I could tell by the look in his eyes that he was terrified, so I tried petting him to calm him down a bit. When I assured myself his heartbeat was near normal again, I knew it was time to leave for the auction sale.

I opened the car door and softly placed the cat on the front seat next to me, all the while petting him profusely until he was purring. All was well. Then...I turned on the ignition. Mistake Number One. One minute the cat was quietly purring beside me on the front seat, and the next he was leaping over the seat into the back of the car and up onto the rear window ledge.

I slowly turned the car onto the highway and started off, all the while looking into the rear view mirror for the cat. All I could see was the cat zipping back and forth across the back window – moving at a speed like a rocket out of hell – then nothing! He had disappeared. Instinct told me to keep going. Wait until you get to the arena and then look for him, I told myself.

At the arena, I opened the car door slightly, afraid that the cat would come barreling out, but he didn't. I still couldn't see him. How could a black cat with a big red bow disappear so fast, I thought. I knew he was in the car somewhere!

Then I looked under the car seat and saw what I thought was his tail. I pulled...and pulled...but he was stuck. Finally, after I pulled a bit more, I retrieved the cat, his eyes bulging out of his head with fear. I picked him up and began petting him until, eventually, he started purring again. Now it was time...

I took him into the arena where a group of children were sitting in a circle. When they saw him with his big red bow, they all wanted to pet him. So I passed the cat to one of the children and, like a game of musical cats, they passed him around from one child to the next. I could see terror mounting in the cat's eyes! But I said nothing, all the while hoping someone would put a bid on him.

Finally, a 12-year-old boy, after much pestering, persuaded his mother to let him buy the cat – for $10. After his Mom doled out the ten bucks, the boy cradled the cat in his arms and took him outside, with the other children in close pursuit.

Once outside, the boy must have decided it was time for the cat to "do his thing" and set it on the ground. Well, once those furry little feet touched the ground, he took off – fur flying in the wind – and that was the last anyone saw of it.

I'm sure that someone in Listowel, preferably a cat lover, found a scrawny, black cat wearing a big red bow, took pity on him, and let him in. And, hopefully, they gave him a name.

38

1990

In 1990, Lorne held a variety of jobs. He continued working for a while for Donkers Harris until things got slack and they let him go. He then went to work for about eight weeks at Ideal Supply Company Ltd., putting in shelving and moving stock around while they added a new addition to their plant. He was only hired there though until the addition was built, then was unemployed again.

About a couple months after leaving Ideal Supply, Lorne was working out in the garage one day when, unexpectedly, Mark F., a guy who Lorne had never seen before, walked into the garage and asked Lorne if he would be interested in working for him. He said he was in charge of starting up a company called First Choice and was told that Lorne was a good worker and had a Millwright's license. So Lorne started there on November 1, 1990, and eventually worked there for 6 ½ years before he retired for good from the work force.

In December, 1990, I finally got Mom moved from Caressant Care in Harriston to Listowel, which was a big plus for me, because I hated winter driving at any time and the road into Harriston could be treacherous in the winter. Not only that though, it was so much closer for me to visit her in Listowel, and I could spend more time with her there.

By this time, Mom's health had deteriorated to the point that she had to be fed, so I wanted to be sure that I was there at supper to feed her since the nurses, as caring as they were, were too rushed to feed the residents properly. I was told by one of the nurses that they (the nurses) were supposed to have all the residents in and out of the dining area in one hour's time.

All the residents at Mom's table needed feeding, which took about an hour just to feed them. And generally, with only two or maybe three nurses on duty at a time, to get them all fed in one hour was an impossibility. Many times I saw residents whisked back to their room and put into bed (at only six o'clock!) with only a few mouthfuls of food in them. I always tried to feed the women that sat at the table with Mom, but it was sad to see some of them taken back to their room on an almost empty stomach. I always stayed with Mom after supper for a while then, so they wouldn't put her in bed. It always infuriated me when they did that because Mom had always been a real night hawk before, and now they wanted her in bed by 6 p.m.

I always felt so sorry for the elderly residents that had no family to speak up for them or to visit them. It is very sad when one works his/ her whole life and then winds up in a nursing home without family or friends to visit.

39

Pastimes and Hobbies

Back in 1987, while still living on the farm, two women from the Listowel area – Lynda Alexander and Doris Erb – organized the Creative Needle Club because they felt there was a need for a sewing club in this area.

Well, I went to the first meeting and joined, and now, 17 years later, the club is still going strong. We hold meetings once a month and enjoy a wide range of activities such as crafts, home decorating, going on bus trips to the Needle Craft Festival in Toronto and to fashion shows, quilt shows, etc. From time to time, we also have speakers come to our club. Every September, the start of another year for our club, we enjoy a potluck supper and, at Christmas, we usually enjoy a catered meal.

In 1989, I was elected to write the news for the club and today, 15 years later, I am still writing it, although I have threatened to quit, but no one wants the job. I've told the President of the club that I would like to be able to just come to a meeting and enjoy it without having to make notes all evening. Every time there's an election though, no one volunteers for the job, then everyone proceeds to tell me what a fine job I'm doing...blah, blah, blah...so I wind up doing it for another year. But once it's written and in *The Listowel Banner*, I think to myself, "Well, that wasn't so hard after all." And even after 15 years, I still enjoy seeing my byline in print.

Last year, our club decided that to get to know everyone, we would all write a one-page biography and put them altogether in a book. The following is my short biography:

BIOGRAPHY OF BEV VOLLMER

I grew up in Kitchener, Ontario. My husband and I married on June 13, 1953, and we lived in Kitchener for 4½ years before buying a farm and moving to the Listowel area on Hwy. 86 between Dorking and Tralee. We raised beef cattle mostly and a few pigs. We farmed for thirty years before we sold the farm in 1989 and moved to 580 Maple Avenue North in Listowel.

I love it here in town and would never want to return to farming – too much work – and I never could get used to that manure smell. Yuk! And I love the convenience of living in town. If you need something at the store or want to go to Tim Horton's for a coffee, you just hop in your car and are there in a matter of minutes, regardless of the weather. When we lived on the farm, there were times in the winter when we were storm bound at home for days, which could get really depressing, with five bored and fighting kids at home!

The special people in my life are my husband and children; we had five, but lost a son to cancer in 1996. A special day for me is June 13, the day my husband and I were married. This year, 2003, we'll be celebrating our 50th anniversary.

My favourite pet is my lovable dog, Fergie, a six-year-old sheltie, sometimes referred to as a Shetland sheep dog. One of her tricks is to say her prayers before she goes to sleep at night (on a blanket beside our bed.)

She folds her paws across each other and waits for me to say, "Good dog!" before she releases them; she then eagerly waits for a treat. She keeps me fit because I have to talk her every day.

My favourite food is homemade soup – I love it! My most despised food is turnip. I never did – and never will – like it!

Most of my Creative Needle friends know that my favourite hobby is making bears. If I didn't have housework to do, I think I'd be in my sewing room all day making them. My husband says that when I'm in my sewing room, it's like I'm in another world – and I guess I am – because when I'm creating a bear, I can forget everything else. I just pop in a CD of my favourite songs and start sewing away. I also love knitting, bowling and gardening. Two years ago, we ripped up our front lawn and made it into a flower garden. I've never regretted it. It's a lot of work but, as the saying goes, it's a labour of love.

I worked part time at *The Listowel Banner* for many years as a typesetter, but am retired now. I now work one morning a week for the VON as a volunteer seniors' fitness instructor at Parkview Gardens on Wednesday mornings, at 10:30 – only $1. Want to come out? (Just had to put in a plug for that!)

My one goal in life is to finish writing my autobiography, one which I started when I retired in 1998. I want to try and finish it for our 50th anniversary this year, and then have books made for each of my four children and 10 grandchildren. I'm now on Chapter 27. It's a slow process though, as I suffer from writer's block quite frequently. I doubt if I'll get it done on time, but I'll keep plugging away anyway until I reach the finish line.

Being a member of the Listowel Creative Needle

Club has been an enjoyable experience for me. I've been a member since its inception and have made a few friends along the way, besides learning some interesting new crafts. I still haven't mastered crocheting though. It's on my list!

***

Besides my Creative Needle Club, I enjoy gardening. A few years ago, I talked Lorne into roto-tilling our front yard and putting in a flower garden. I first made a rough design on paper though before we started, so I would have some idea of what I wanted. Lorne is my right-hand man – does the heavy work; I do the planting and weeding (and a lot of bending!).

Last year, I sure was surprised when we received an envelope in the mail with the return address from The Town of North Perth. My first reaction was *Damn! Another tax bill already!* Then I looked more closely at the envelope and it read: L. Vollmer, Communities in Bloom Front Lawn 1st Prize Winner. Inside was an invitation for us to attend a wine and cheese social in the library and also a barbecue at the home of David and Rosemary Galloway, owners of Listowel Landscaping. Lorne and I attended both. We also won a $100 gift certificate from Listowel Landscaping. A great gift! The funny part of it all though was that we never entered the contest; our mailman had submitted our names.

Another pastime I enjoy is knitting. As I have to be doing something when I'm watching TV, I like to keep my knitting bag handy in the livingroom for those times I sit down in front of the tube. I generally knit for an hour or so every night while I watch the news.

Another hobby of mine, as you've already learned from my one-page autobiography, is making stuffed teddy bears. I have sold a few over the years, but mostly just make them for the sheer enjoyment I get from seeing a bear completed. I make them for my church's spring and fall social, as door prizes for the penny booth. I've also made them for birthday and Christmas gifts. I made one last year for the Seniors'

Christmas party for their silent auction. (Lorne and I are members.) Occasionally, I make angel bears for my son's clients whenever one of them has a baby. On the angel's wings, I embroider the baby's name and birth date. I've also knit many bears, too.

Bowling was also a pastime that I've enjoyed very much over the years, even winning a few trophies now and then. But the bowling alley in Listowel closed a few years ago, and I haven't bowled since.

40

Time Capsule

In 1999, I made a teddy bear for our family reunion. In it, I inserted a time capsule with the following letter.

March 16, 1999

Dear Descendant:

The year is 1999. In about nine months from now, we will be approaching the new millennium, the year 2000. I've left instructions to open the time capsule in this bear in the year 2100. Hopefully, my bear will last that long.

What will life be like a hundred years from now, I can't even visualize. Will there be electric cars by then? Will people travel to other planets for a summer holiday? Will people be cloned? Will couples have a choice on the sex of their children? Will children still attend school or will they receive their schooling at home through the internet? Will a cure be found for diseases such as cancer, diabetes or multiple sclerosis? (People seem to be dying today in epidemic proportions from cancer.) Will people travel back and forth to work in space vehicles? Or maybe they won't have to go to work at all, maybe all the work will be done on computers from home. Few people live to be in their

90s today, and even few live beyond 100. Will people's lifespan increase by the year 2100? Who knows.

Although many of these questions seem far-fetched at the present, in a hundred years from now, many of these things could be possible. Only you, my descendants, will know the answers to these questions by then.

Just as I question what life will be like in your era, I'm sure you must question what life was like in my era. So let me pass on some tidbits from my time.

- *I remember when my mother occasionally would give me a nickel to spend at the grocery store on a couple of two-cent grab bags (little bags will with candy). She always reminded me to bring home the change. The year was 1943. I was six years old.*
- *I remember another time when I was six or seven and got to ride in the rumble seat of our neighbour's new car. What a thrill that was!*
- *As a kid, the toys I received at Christmas were inexpensive and simple, maybe a doll or plastic tea set and a few inexpensive clothes, but I was excited as could be with every gift I opened.*
- *As a child I remember getting our water from a pump by the sink in the kitchen. The water had to be heated. Once a week (on Saturday nights), we kids (my brother and I) got a bath in a galvanized tub which my mother brought in from the back shanty and set in the kitchen. We had to take turns bathing in the same water. We had no plumbing in the house at all, which meant no bathroom, just a pail under the bed for emergencies.*
- *I attended a four-room school, two grades to a class. (My husband attended a one-room school, eight grades in one!)*
- *In 1952, when I was 14, I landed my first job at the Dominion Electro-home in Kitchener, wiring radios. I was later promoted to wiring TVs. My husband and I owned the first television on our street when we were first married, and it was only in black and white. When the first coloured TV came out, the colour was terrible for the first few years.*
- *When I started school, King George VI reigned as King. Queen Elizabeth came next. Her coronation took place in June, 1953, the same year and*

month that my husband and I were married. That year, my dad owned
a 1931 Model A Ford and my husband owned a 1940 Ford Mercury.

• In the early years of our marriage, I did all my laundry in a wringer
washing machine, first filling up the machine with water and then filling up the rinse tub. All the clothes had to be put through the wringer
and then hung out to dry on the clothesline. No automatic dryers back
then. I got my first automatic washer and dryer around 1975, when my
youngest was about 12 years old. We had cloth diapers back then, too,
which we rinsed in the toilet and then put in a pail to soak until wash
day. No disposable diapers back then!

• My husband and I moved from Kitchener, Ontario, to a farm in Listowel
in the spring of 1958, with three children in tow. We had no bathroom
in the house for the first year; we had to use a pail (yuk!) which we kept
upstairs in one of the bedrooms. It had to be taken out daily (sometimes
oftener) and dumped at the end of the garden. That area was a terrible
sight in the spring after the snow was gone until my husband got it
plowed. It sure felt wonderful when we finally got the bathroom in.

• Two more children eventually arrived after moving to the farm. Money
was tight in the early years of our marriage so I bought "surprise"
packages of fabric through Eaton's and Sears' catalogues (because it was
cheaper that way) and then made the fabric into clothes for the kids.
I found it a real challenge (but fun) deciding what to make with each
piece of fabric.

• Back in 1953, butter was 59 cents a pound. Today, 1999, it is around $3
a pound. A dozen eggs now cost $1.89; ten pounds of potatoes $2.49; ten
pounds of apples $4.99; or three MacIntosh apples 58 cents; bananas 69
cents a pound; a litre of milk $1.99; 2.4 kg of laundry detergent $4.99.

• At present, Bill Clinton is President of the United States, but a scan-
dalous affair with an intern, Monica Lewinsky, is causing worldwide
attention. At the present time, the Republicans are trying to have him
impeached, although the majority of people want him to stay. So he had
an affair, he is still an excellent President, they say.

If you, the reader, have waited until 2100 to read this, then I thank you *for waiting and hope you have found enjoyment in these few tidbits of my life. Although I will have long disappeared off the face of the earth by then, I feel I have left a bit of myself behind in this letter and also in my bear. (I hope it stayed intact until 2100.)*

May God bless you in your lifetime,

Your friend and ancestor,

Beverly J. Vollmer
Born Oct 28, 1937

P.S. I've included a few extra little tidbits in the time capsule which I thought one would find interesting 100 years from now.

41

And Now

Lorne and I have been in town now for fifteen years and although we no longer live the hectic pace we once did on the farm, we are still very active and haven't retired to our rocking chairs as yet. Hopefully, our health won't deteriorate for a while, as we still have many things we want to do.

Lorne is very involved in the Junior B hockey team here in town and, until this year, has been on the executive. He has helped do everything over the years from selling tickets at the door to running the bar during their Friday night hockey games to helping build a dressing room for the players. Four years ago, at the end-of-the-year Junior B banquet, Lorne was presented with a trophy which read:

Listowel Jr. B Cyclones Dedication Award Presented to Lorne Vollmer

1999-2000

In my opinion, he really deserved it because, at times, it seemed he was at the arena more than he was at home.

Lorne also keeps busy around the yard in the summer as my right-hand man in the garden and fixing things around the house when they break down, such as the vacuum cleaner. I think he has saved us a fortune in just repairing that one appliance! Whenever one of their toys break, Brett and Kelsey, two of our grandchildren usually always bring it to Grandpa to fix. In their young minds, Lorne is the "Grandpa who can fix anything."

I'm also very busy since moving to town. That old saying about "a woman's work is never done" is so true. When you live in a house, there is always work to be done, always something to clean! (Dust accumulates quite quickly whether one lives in the country or in town.) And in the summer, especially, I am very busy with my front-yard garden, cleaning windows, painting, etc.

Besides my Creative Needle Club, which meets once a month, I work as a volunteer for the VON as a Senior Lifestyle Instructor for a seniors' exercise class held every Wednesday morning at Parkview Gardens. It's a "seniors-helping-seniors" group. As well as keeping me in shape, I feel in some small way I'm also contributing to keeping other seniors fit.

And, also, just recently I joined the horticultural society here in town. We meet once a month to discuss subjects relating to gardening, etc. The first meeting I attended was about roses, and the most recent one was on photographing your garden.

Other interests of mine are reading (whenever I get a chance), and walking my dog, Fergie.

Now that we are in town, Lorne and I have a bit more time to travel, too. We have been to Las Vegas quite a few times, even winning a bit (believe it or not!). Other places we have travelled to are Florida, Wheeling, Nashville, Branson, and New York City (which I hated!). And in a few weeks, we're going to Atlantic City for four days to take in a few shows and maybe do a bit of gambling. Hopefully, we'll win a bit – or maybe lose the kids' inheritance – but I hope not! Last year, we went on a Mystery Trip for five days, which turned out to be a very nice holiday near Peterborough.

We also go on many day trips, via bus, with the seniors, sometimes to see a play and sometimes to visit Casino Niagara or Casino Rama. Whatever we do, we never seem to get bored.

I wish I could say life has been all sunshine and roses since moving to town, but there have been dark clouds too. Mom passed away on January 17, 1995, at age 82 – six years after we came to town. And on August 8, 1996, our son Mike passed away from cancer (lymphoma). The only thing, I think, that kept me from falling to pieces after Mike died was my belief that someday we will meet again. A few years ago while Lorne was away on a fishing trip, I even bought a cemetery plot next to Mike's grave. My one wish is to be buried in the grave next to him.

I have never been a deeply religious person, but I do believe in God and the hereafter, and agree with Eugene Cernan, who wrote in *The Last Man on the Moon:* "No one in his right mind can see such a sight [as stars in the night sky] and deny the existence of a supreme being. [...]. It is just too perfect and beautiful to have happened by accident."

***

Last year, Lorne and I celebrated our 50th wedding anniversary and, hopefully, we have many more to come.

Do I have any regrets about my life? Yes, two! I regret never going to university and getting an English degree, and I regret never having attended a high school reunion.

I started this autobiography in 1998, now it is 2004. I am glad it is coming to an end. Whether anyone will read it or not is another story, but I feel fulfilled in FINALLY finishing it. Donna asked me recently, "When do we get to read it?" Hopefully, the answer will be this Christmas, which now is only three weeks away. But, maybe not!

An added note here: Charin gave birth to a baby boy on September 27 of this year (2004). That was my brother's birthday. (What a coincidence, huh?) Charin and husband, Greg, now have three sons – Kelsey, Brett and Sammy (Donald).

I would like to leave the following item with my children that I clipped form the newspaper a few years ago. Although I never wrote the article, it expresses my sentiments exactly:

My dear children,

I love you very much and I know you love me. This is the way I have planned the rest of my life, and I hope you will honour my wishes.

I intend to live in my home until taking care of it is more than I am able to do. I will then move into a small apartment. When I need to be cared for, I will enter an adult-care home. When I say, "This is what I want," I mean it. You may think I am stubborn, but please think of me as being determined.

I am now 67 years of age [I changed the age to my own] *and you know that I have had a wonderful life. I don't want to spoil yours. I insist that you live yours to the hilt. Travel! Enjoy yourselves! I do not want to move in with any of you. Please don't try to talk me into it. These are my orders and I insist that you follow them. I love you all very much.*

Your mother

P.S. I also never want to go on life support – let me die in peace.

42

Parting Messages

MISS ME BUT LET ME GO
Christina Rosetti (1830-1894).

When I come to the end of the road
And the sun has set for me,
I want no rights in a gloom-filled room
Why cry for a soul set free.
Miss me a little, but not too long
And not with your head bowed low,
Remember the love we once shared
Miss me but let me go.
For this is the journey we all must take
And each must go alone,
It's all a part of the Master's plan
A step on the road to home.
When you are lonely and sick at heart
Go to the friends we know,
And bury your sorrows in doing good deeds
Miss me, but let me go.

***

Death, the one appointment we all must keep, and for which no time is set.
-- Charlie Chan

Editor's Epilogue

Dad died in 2011. After being married for 57½ years, life for Mom without Dad was lonely at first. Mom sold the house on Maple Avenue and moved into a condo on Leisure Lane. (The official address was Nelson Avenue, but there was an actual sign with the name Leisure Lane.) She loved her condo with its small garden by the front door, where she would putter, planting cosmos seeds, coaxing a Rose of Sharon to bloom, and cursing the weeds. Mom was never without a dog, so there was a little patio out the back with enough green grass to allow Fergie, then Sadie, to do her business. Mom soon had a circle of friends to go for dinner or an afternoon coffee at Tim's.

About seven years later, Mom was diagnosed with early to middle stage Alzheimer's. At first, we stepped up the frequency of our visits, but eventually Mom could no longer live on her own. She moved, dog in tow, to London, Ontario, with me and my husband. After three years here, she passed away in October, 2022.

During the caregiving years, I wrote of our experiences and created tales about her teddy bears, most of whom also had Alzheimer's. I wove together Mom's writings and mine with the bear stories to create a memoir – *If I Could Remember, I Would: Teddy Bears & Brains & Caring for my Mother*.

Mom enjoyed poetry, such as "Miss Me But Let Me Go" in the last chapter that she used to conclude her *Autobiography*. But tucked in the back of the green binder she had once given me were several other poems, including "An Old Lady's Poem," said to have been found by a nurse in a care home at Ashlauie Hospital, Dundee, Scotland. That the poem was special to Mom is obvious, as she had it laminated. In the poem, an old woman in a nursing home speaks to the nurses who don't see the child, the young teen, the mother, or all the other roles the old woman has lived. The poem ends:

> *So open your eyes, nurse, open and see*
> *Not a crabby old woman; look closer...see ME!!*

I hope this Autobiography, and my memoir, help you see Beverly not just as my mother but as the unique soul that she was.

Love you, Mom.

Donna Costa
London, Ontario
April 2023

Editor's Acknowledgements

Many thanks to Beverly Vollmer (my mother) for writing her autobiography many years ago. Her stories are a treasure for me and all her descendants. Putting her words into a format for publishing has been a legacy project that has been healing in many ways. It's been an honour to complete what she started and I am so very proud that her published life story will forever be housed in the National Archives of Canada. Mom, you are gone, but never forgotten.

This book could not have been published without the cooperation of my siblings and their spouses – Brian and Lynda, Bill and Deb, Charin and Greg. Thanks for being my family through thick and thin.

Thank you to the indefatigable Susan L. Scott for believing in this project and cheering me on to the finish line.

And finally, thanks to my husband, Ang, who stood by me when the going got tough.

Editor's Bio

DONNA COSTA is the third and middle child of Beverly Vollmer's five children.

A writer like her mother, Costa's debut novel of young adult fiction, *Breathing With Trees*, was released in 2020. Her creative non-fiction appears in literary magazines and is regularly shortlisted in contests. Those stories and more are featured in her memoir, *If I Could Remember, I Would: Brains & Bears & Caring For My Mother.*

Donna lives with her husband in a den of her mother's teddy bears in London, Ontario.